D0848918

Crossing Over

Affirmations of Faith in the Midst of the Dying

JUNE E. KUYKENDALL, RN, BSN, CHPN

A Nurse's Journey of Faith While Working with the Terminally Ill

WESTBOW
PRESS®
A DIVISION OF THOMAS NELSON
& ZONDERVAN

This book is a work of non-fiction. Unless otherwise noted, the author and the publisher make no explicit guarantees as to the accuracy of the information contained in this book and in some cases, names of people and places have been altered to protect their privacy.

Scripture taken from the King James Version of the Bible.

People and incidents in this book are created by the author from her experience in dealing with patients at the end of life. Most names and details have been changed to protect the privacy of those involved, and any similarity between actual names and stories and those described in this book is purely coincidental. Real names have been used only with written permission of the family.

WestBow Press books may be ordered through booksellers or by contacting:

WestBow Press
A Division of Thomas Nelson & Zondervan
1663 Liberty Drive
Bloomington, IN 47403
www.westbowpress.com
1 (866) 928-1240

Because of the dynamic nature of the Internet, any web addresses or links contained in this book may have changed since publication and may no longer be valid. The views expressed in this work are solely those of the author and do not necessarily reflect the views of the publisher, and the publisher hereby disclaims any responsibility for them.

Any people depicted in stock imagery provided by Thinkstock are models, and such images are being used for illustrative purposes only. Certain stock imagery © Thinkstock.

ISBN: 978-1-5127-3799-8 (sc)
ISBN: 978-1-5127-3800-1 (hc)
ISBN: 978-1-5127-3798-1 (e)

Library of Congress Control Number: 2016905976

Print information available on the last page.

WestBow Press rev. date: 04/14/2016

Contents

This book is lovingly dedicated to my husband, Larry Kuykendall, who was the driving force in my writing of these stories. I also want to dedicate this book to all of my patients who, over the years, have blessed me and made my faith journey with God more meaningful.

Acknowledgments

I want to express my gratitude to my Savior and His Holy Spirit who has been beside me in all paths that I have walked. Without His guiding force, none of this would have been possible. Thank you to my daughter, Renee, who added enlightenment to these stories. Last, thanks to my pastor, Daryl Dunsmore, who encouraged me many times and who showed an interest in this topic.

1

Personal Reflection of Faith

The restful night was shattered by the ringing of the telephone, signaling that someone needed the services of this palliative care nurse. Glancing at the clock, I saw it was 2:00 a.m., and after reassuring my husband that I would be close by tonight, I slipped out into the crisp, cool air. Thankful that I only had a few miles to go, I ushered up a prayer: "God, give me the strength and knowledge to handle whatever has caused the distress in my patient."

Terry

Terry, my fifty-year-old patient, was experiencing the same hallucination again, which his caregiver and significant other couldn't handle, and the patient wanted his nurse—that being me—to come to assess him. After arriving, I found Terry sitting straight up in bed (he had been bed-bound for the past several weeks), very distraught, wide-eyed, and pointing to the corner of his bedroom.

"Can't you see him?" he shouted.

The man in the long black cape with a hood, motioning for him to follow, had appeared again, disrupting Terry's peace of mind. Scrambling for answers, I started assessing for possibilities. *Must be the narcotic he has been taking—but wait; it's been several days since Terry chose to stop taking the narcotics. The cancer must have metastasized to his brain, but no; his form of cancer doesn't metastasize to the brain. Must be having pain. No, he denies that it is a physical pain.* Quickly, I attempted to calm him down by asking why he thought this kept happening, particularly in the early hours of the morning.

Terry had not been religious per se; according to him, he didn't have time for such nonsense. Church was not a part of his life because he never saw the need to go where there were a bunch of hypocrites acting like they were better than everyone else. His military background had made him hard and tough, and he believed he could handle anything that came his way. I had heard this many times before from him and knew I had to approach this topic again very carefully so as not to jeopardize his confidence in and ease with me. Whispering quietly, I said, "God, help me be strong."

Very boldly, I again questioned, "Why do you think this keeps happening?"

Almost inaudibly and with tears streaming down his face, he answered, "Because I am living in sin and not married to this woman."

Even in this state of duress, he knew he needed something more. He knew at that moment that there was the real possibility of a heaven and a hell. He needed to choose whom he wanted to serve—God or Satan. The Evil One was calling him night after night from the corner of his bedroom.

This night, I didn't need to give physical medicine to ease his pain because he needed medicine of a different kind—a spiritual kind. Thankfully, I had that type of medicine to share. I talked about my walk with Christ, how He loves us no matter what we have done in the past, and that we can become a new creature in Him.

"Do you want that assurance, Terry?" I asked very quietly.

"Yes, if it's not too late," he answered, so soft and low that at first I wasn't certain he had even spoken.

But his eyes showed an anticipation I had not seen in him for weeks. After the sinner's prayer was repeated, he gave his heart to the Lord and expressed his desire to marry his girlfriend before God called him home. This goal was accomplished through a godly minister and legal help from local facilities.

God always clears obstacles from the path when He is bringing one into the fold. Terry died two weeks later without seeing that black-hooded man again. The Holy Spirit is alive and continues to abate the forces of evil. An affirmation of faith that God is in control was established again in my heart.

I believe God has a purpose for everyone who is born into this world, and that purpose can have a negative or a positive influence on others, depending on how one chooses to use it. As a small child, my dream was to become a nurse, but circumstances beyond my control did not allow this dream to become a reality until many years later, after marriage and a teenage daughter. God had a purpose for me, but He wanted me to wait. The reason for the delay may have been that He wanted me to find a godly, supportive man who wanted the best for me, just as He, my heavenly Father, desired for me.

Being poor and experiencing hardships went hand and hand in our home. Raised by godly parents, I was taught the importance of hard work and to be thankful to God, our provider, for all things, even when our hearts didn't feel like being grateful. "God will always provide" was my mother's motto, despite her having to do without many comforts that others took for granted. My mind still clings to vivid memories, as if it were only yesterday, of huddling around the old coal stove while snow blew through the cracks under the door, with Mother focused intently on reading from the family Bible. Despite money being scarce, Dad would give what was due to the Lord, oftentimes giving extra to a neighbor who needed help. When I questioned his reasoning behind this when I needed new shoes or a new dress, he would say that this was our "seed faith" at work.

I certainly didn't understand about seed faith when all my friends at school had new sneakers or new clothes. Hand-me-downs did not make me one of the popular girls at school, particularly when the one who handed the clothes down to me was a classmate. Hebrews 13:5 ("Let your conversation be without covetousness and be content with such things as you have ...") certainly had no significance to me at the time.

My faith was built through those formative years. This seed faith never became clearer to me than when my parents experienced illnesses that required multiple hospitalizations. I experienced heightened anxiety and fear of an uncertain future. God's Word rang in my head: "For he hath said I will never leave thee, nor forsake thee" (Hebrews 13:5). We stood on that promise. Neighbors and friends stopped by to lend a hand, gave monetary gifts, brought food, or just relayed words of encouragement. Dad reminded me, when I had become a grown woman, that this was the seed faith at work that he had planted years ago. Wow! He was right all along, just as our heavenly Father is always right. This was an affirmation of faith that would sustain me in the years to come.

When God is in the plans for your life, He will go before you to prepare the way when you feel there is no way or when you have a fear of just stepping out into the unknown. I had many examples put before me where God made the way. Throughout all the obstacles of caring for my invalid parents until their deaths, the burning desire to help others never left me, and in fact, it became even more of a yearning when my daughter went to college to pursue her dreams. I wondered, *Is it my time, God? In Your Word it says, "To everything there is a season and a time to every purpose under the heaven" (Ecclesiastes 3:1). Is this my season?* My husband felt that it was my time and a long overdue season.

God opened the way for me to be accepted to a Christian college where His Word was incorporated into all fields of study. Spirituality in academia was very important at this four-year college. With a three-hour round-trip commute each day, I had a great deal of time to talk with God about what His plans for me would be in the future. My faith continued to grow because in this college atmosphere I was allowed to talk to colleagues and professors about the Lord and how He was my strength in all things. The curriculum required that I be involved in community service projects as well as a cross-culture experience (going to another country for service), which demonstrated the poverty and hardships sustained by others in Third World countries. During these experiences, one soon realizes that people with horrific and preventable diseases could be saved if medicine and clean drinking water were available. Many were persecuted for their faith in Jesus Christ by being maimed or killed. This experience only created more of a burning desire to become the Christian nurse God had planned for me. I might not get to serve in another country, but God had a purpose for me wherever He would lead me. The verse came loud and clear in my head: "Inasmuch as ye have done it unto one of the least of these my brethren, ye have done it unto me" (Matthew 25:40). The least of these can be in your own community.

Being a "nontraditional" student meant that I was a little older than the normal college student, but God tempered the hearts of my young colleagues to respect and accept me in every part of the curriculum. "God is good, all the time—all the time God is good." How many times had I heard this growing up?

Graduation was the highlight of my life. Not only had God granted traveling safety for the four years of commuting, but He had allowed me to graduate with honors. His Word is truth. "Beloved I wish above all things that thou mayest prosper and be in health, even as thy soul prospereth" (3 John 2). He wants to be involved in every aspect of our lives.

Equipped with nursing skills and a New Testament Bible stuffed in the pocket of my white uniform, I set out to spread my compassion and ability to the injured and afflicted. The assessment skills and practice that I had been taught proved to be easier to achieve than the ability to practice my faith in an emergency room or the critical care facility where I had been placed. The Lord's Word from the passage of 3 John 5 went through my head often: "Beloved, thou doest faithfully whatsoever thou doest to the brethren, and to strangers." *But God, I don't have time in these environments* was the silent answer I gave each time this verse entered my head. The opportunity never presented itself to share how important one's faith needs to be when death can come at any minute in these settings.

I have heard it said that all good things come to those who wait, and that opportunity came when I began working with the dying through hospice care. This was an anointed call to minister in the physical as well as in the spiritual sense. Hospice had a major impact on my walk with God that brought some of the brightest and some of the darkest journeys. For twenty-plus years, I worked as a nurse in end-of-life care. Many times over those years, people questioned why I chose to stay in this area of nursing. "Isn't it depressing or stressful?" they would ask. My reply came very quickly: I had been blessed with the God-given opportunity to be in the presence of the dying. I was allowed a glimpse of what is in store for us when that last breath is taken. Being present at some of these was glorious, while some who passed became troubling in my spirit. One of my favorite sayings to my nurses that I supervised was "This is where the rubber meets the road." There are no second chances when one draws that final breath; it will be either heaven or hell. I will always be grateful to those saints who let me have a small part in that transition from this life to their eternal life. My faith was strengthened by their sharing of what they saw as they crossed over.

"And we know that all things work together for good to them that love God, to them who are called according to his purpose" (Romans 8:28).

2

Is Heaven Real? Patients Who Have Affirmed That Heaven Does Exist

Olivia

God puts people in your path who have such a profound impact on your life that you can only trust in His grace about what is happening around you. A colleague of mine, Dean, often shared the beautiful antics of his two children and his plans for their future. One of those children was Olivia, a beautiful blonde, blue-eyed four-year–old who had such energy that her dad had difficulty keeping up with her pranks with her older brother.

Early one morning when Dean came to work, he entered my office to chat. That was somewhat unusual, and I also noticed a change in his appearance. Over the weekend, Olivia had experienced a severe headache and ataxia (uncoordinated walking). In a short time, those beautiful blue eyes became crossed, and her vision became unfocused.

Quickly, a diagnosis confirmed that she had a neuroblastoma in her brain stem—a very rapid-growing malignancy. The tumor was inoperable. In my spirit, I cried out and asked God, *Why are You allowing this to happen?* Dean was raising his children in God's shadow, and he had been serving the Lord for many years. It wasn't fair.

I was reminded of the Bible prophet Job, who had served God in all ways, but Satan was allowed to take everything from him—family, friends, health, possessions—and still he continued to serve God. At the end of Job's trials, he came to realize that God is all-powerful and all-knowing. Was God allowing the Evil One to torment this family, just as He had allowed persecutions to come upon Job?

Doctors who had experience with this disease soon suggested to Olivia's family that chemotherapy might be the only option that could extend her life. All of Dean's faith was put in this option, and he knew that God would use this avenue to cure Olivia; God had bigger plans. Family and friends prayed daily for her healing, but healing came through a different method. God always heals the faithful, but many times it isn't the way we expect it to come.

Throughout the process of their long trips for the treatments and shorter spans between hospitalizations, Olivia's little body began to change. She experienced weakness and shortness of breath, causing her to be oxygen-dependent due to the increased edema from the disease and causing stroke-like symptoms on her right side. She asked, "Daddy, why won't this dumb old arm work anymore?" It was difficult for this child to comprehend what was happening to her small body. Soon, she was unable to walk and had to be carried. *God where are you now when this family needs you?*

I thought. *In Isaiah 53:5 it says, "And with His stripes we are healed." Why hasn't your healing come?*

Soon, Olivia's physician gave her only a few months to live. That Christmas was to be her last with her earthly family. By the next Christmas, she would be celebrating Christ's birthday in His presence. Beautiful Olivia died during the winter, when all things appear drab and dreary. She was just five years old; a bright light gone from our presence. God healed her at her crossing over. We don't always understand why death has to happen to the innocent and the pure, but as I am reminded in God's Word, "and sendeth rain on the just and on the unjust" (Matthew 5:45).

Dean became more withdrawn but eventually began to share things as God revealed them to him in his dreams and memories. . Reflecting back over the year prior to Olivia's illness, Dean remembered that he had often heard Olivia talking in her bedroom to someone whom he had assumed was an imaginary playmate. She called the playmate Jesus. On a few occasions, he would hear her laughing and dancing around, and when asked what she was doing, she replied with a smile, "I am dancing with my angel, Daddy." God had revealed to a child what He had in store for her. God reveals Himself to children because they are still pure in heart and are open for the supernatural, whereas adults become cynical and closed-hearted.

Jesus said, "Suffer little children, and forbid them not, to come unto me; for of such is the kingdom of heaven" (Matthew 19:14).

This passing brought more questions. Is God real? Is heaven real? Will we see Olivia again? Olivia touched our lives for a brief moment but long enough to affirm that Jesus is real and has a real place waiting for us to be reunited with our faithful loved ones who have passed on. The affirmation of my faith was again confirmed by a five-year-old child's acceptance of life after death. How awesome it must have been for her to cross over with her playful angel carrying her to her heavenly home.

Preacher Smith

Preacher Smith touched my heart long before he became my patient. He had been my pastor for many years and had been a wonderful mentor to my husband and me. Sharing the gospel with this man was one of the highlights of our visits to his home. His life was to be shortened by bladder cancer that he fought for many years, and it soon became apparent that he was losing the battle, despite multiple prayers for his healing.

I never heard him question why God hadn't healed him. He was a workaholic for God and didn't have time for illness during those thirty-one years as our pastor; he didn't even take a vacation. "Vacation" was spent working at Saint Jude's Hospital. Eventually, he did have to make time for this disease, which weakened his body but not his spirit. Choosing to remain at home with his godly wife of many years and to be surrounded by his daughter and her family, he requested hospice care. His daughter was a registered nurse who was very instrumental in his care, but at this point she realized she needed to be the daughter rather than the nurse. This was my time to be that nurse and minister to him, as he had so often done for my family over the years.

The savagery of cancer soon took control of his body, confining him to bed. On each visit, we continued to share about the Lord and what was in store for him. Our visits ended each time with his requesting that I lift up a prayer for him. It was so gratifying to me that now he believed in the power of my prayers. On one occasion, I was very surprised when he asked me if I really believed in heaven. Why was he asking me this question when for thirty-one years he had preached in his sermons about this place prepared for us? "What if all these years, I have been wrong and there isn't anything after this?" he sadly asked.

Silently, I prayed, *Oh Lord, help me to say the right thing to this loving servant of Yours. Bring Your words to my lips to ease his distress.*

I remembered Matthew 25:34 ("Then shall the King say unto them on his right hand, Come Ye blessed of my Father, inherit the kingdom prepared for you from the foundation of the world") as well as John 14:2 ("In My Father's house are many mansions. If it were not so, I would have told you. I go to prepare a place for you").

These words slipped easily off my tongue to a man who had shared those same Scriptures from the pulpit many times. He smiled at these words as if I had just passed a test. Was he testing me to see if I would be able to tell others who doubted that something more was out there? The topic never came up again between us. Either he was at peace—if indeed he truly had questioned a real heaven—or he was satisfied that I had become bolder in my faith and could reach out to others.

During the night when Preacher Smith was crossing over, the family was at his bedside, as they had been many nights in the past, but this particular night was to be like none other. I was blessed to be included in this gathering. Slipping in and out of consciousness, with various times of lucidness, Preacher Smith continued to preach the gospel as he had done for many years. This was to be his greatest and final sermon. He stated, "I have never felt such love and peace as I do right now." He began quoting 2 Timothy 4:7–8. "I have fought the good fight; I have finished my course; I have kept the faith. Henceforth there is laid up for me a crown of righteousness, which the Lord, the righteous Judge, will award to me on this day."

I noticed he had changed the wording to "this day" rather than "that day." Even in Preacher's state of supposed confusion, God was revealing His love to all those present through this man. In his lucid moments, he requested that we sing certain hymns; he had memorized the page numbers from his old, tattered songbook. "Join hands and pray the Lord's Prayer!" he shouted. He spoke with such energy that I knew his strength was coming from God. Preacher's last instruction was to remind the family that they had to carry on the work for the Lord because there was much to do yet. It wasn't long before God called him home.

When I left that night, I realized I had been to a church service like none I had ever attended. God's angels and His Holy Spirit were present in that room while Preacher Smith was being healed in the spiritual sense as he crossed over. Heaven is real; I glimpsed it that night in a man who never doubted that it was out there.

Maybe I needed another affirmation to remove all doubts that there is a wonderful place called heaven waiting for all who are born again through His Son, Jesus. I believe I passed Preacher Smith's test that night.

Many times as nurses, we are caught up in meeting the physical needs of our patients, as well as the psychosocial needs, but it is imperative that we realize that everything can't be fixed with narcotics or anxiety pills. The spiritual pain is often the most overlooked in all health care settings. Instead, we assess the pain and rate it, notifying the physician, who orders the narcotic to be increased (which is appropriate many times), but often the pain continues to increase despite the patient's state of opioid euphoria. It becomes a domino effect—increased restlessness, increased anxiety, increased titration of the narcotic, increased stress to the family. Increases go on and on, and the patient is never comfortable.

Hospice nurses are educated in looking at the whole person, which includes the spiritual needs as well. This part of the nursing assessment is so vital, but it's one in which many nurses do not want to become involved because they are not comfortable in their own spirituality, or they haven't given any thought to the direction of their own faith journey.

By realizing that there is a tangible place called heaven or hell waiting in the balance, nurses can be the bridge that will help secure where that patient—woman or man—will spend eternity. Before death, everyone wants to find meaning in the midst of the dying process. Patients often have a life review if they are coherently able to do so. These are golden moments for nurses and other health care workers when they can listen to the patients' regrets of their past and find out what brings meaning to their lives. It is a time to share that God loves them no matter what happened in the past, and He will forgive them so they can forgive themselves. The crossing of this bridge will allow for a peaceful death. This opens up a path to ease the spiritual pain that often goes untreated in our health care system. The fear of repercussions from employers and colleagues holds many Christian health care workers back. In Christ, there comes boldness with opportunities and open doors to minister to our hurting patients. As nurses, we must be bold in Christ to walk through those open doors. The gratification becomes so meaningful because we have met a need for our patients that no one else may be able to do. Everyone desires—and deserves—a peaceful death when there is no longer a cure, except God's cure.

Our country was founded on religious freedom, but Christians have been stripped of a lot of those freedoms. Fear has entered the health care fields, where to discuss Christ would be infringing upon the patients' rights to freedom of religion. Why is it not possible to question what a person believes and to question why he or she ascribes to that belief? As a nurse, I have never pushed my faith or been intolerant when listening to beliefs that are different from mine, but if the opportunity presented itself, and God opened the door for the topic, I gladly would walk through. In many encounters, my conversation was rebuffed, but the seed was planted, and it was up to God to nurture and water that seed thereafter.

Dad—the Seed Planter

The spirituality component of the dying process became very personal to me on the day that my dad was leaving this physical earth to join my mother, whom he had longed to be with for several years. That day, the nurse in me was doing what nurses do—ministering to the physical needs and not really listening to what was being said from the dying loved one. He was so coherent, refusing any life-sustaining treatments, only wanting to be released from his earthly body that had entrapped him for three long years. The hemorrhaging from his colon, secondary to his end-stage heart disease, continued throughout the day. On several occasions he would point out the window, very excited, saying, "Look at that beautiful crystal sea, Babe. Don't you see it?"

My nursing skills were at work, and I realized he must be very dehydrated and in need of fluids, which he continued to refuse. He waited patiently for my daughter to arrive from college to say his good-bye. Shortly after her arrival, he looked up, smiled, and crossed over to be with Mother.

Weeks later, when the void wasn't as great, my husband questioned why I hadn't continued the conversation with Dad about the crystal sea and why I couldn't understand what he was telling us. A light went off in my head, and my spirit began to grieve as it hadn't done since his death. I realized—too late— that I had missed a wonderful opportunity to talk and share about what my dying dad was seeing on the other side. His body wasn't euphoric from narcotics, nor was he incoherent about what was happening to him. He just wanted to share what God had revealed to him. I remembered the Lord's Prayer; the one I had recited often with my parents as I was growing up. "The Lord is my Shepherd, I shall not want; He leadeth me beside the still waters ... yea though I walk through the valley of the shadow of death, I will fear no evil for thou art with me" (Psalm 23:1–2, 4).

Dad was trying to tell me that there was a place of rest that had a crystal river that flowed from God on high. His storm was about to pass; the crystal sea promised a peace and calmness that was waiting for him. Another glimpse of heaven was revealed to me in my journey for truth, but sadly, it was an opportunity missed. I vowed never to miss another opportunity of what God reveals to the faithful in death.

Through these few stories, one can see that heaven is a real place. Their "hallucinations" can't be explained away by narcotic usage because these patients weren't on any mind-altering medications. The mind-altering effect came from the heavenly Father, who was about to release them from their physical bodies. He was giving them a glimpse into the restful place He had prepared for them.

The scientific community has been quick to explain that there are "chemical imbalances" in the brain that cause the dying to glimpse a mythical realm, but I am a palliative care nurse who has stood by too many bedsides of patients who have described loved ones who have gone on before them for me to believe it's a "chemical imbalance." Many have seen a baby brother or sister that they did not know existed until a member of the family verified this event.

Many examples will be shared throughout this book that verify that heaven is real and can't be explained by nonbelieving, intellectual persons who have not had these experiences or who have refused to listen to what the dying have shared.

These "chemical imbalances" become a source of contention when dealing with patients who have had hallucinatory euphoria that wasn't a positive encounter. These often are not talked about or explained by the scientific-minded. The "bright light, long tunnel" and feelings of euphoria are the chemical imbalances the nonbelievers draw upon as evidence that each dying person experiences these concepts. I beg to differ! I'll reveal a few stories of the darker side, where that didn't occur in the dying process, but these stores will be kept to a minimum since they bring attention to the one who doesn't deserve any glory.

You can be the judge of what to believe—science or deity. If you are going on a faith journey, the ultimate conclusion will be deity if your heart is right with God. If your heart attitude is not right, take a moment right now to ask Christ to forgive those shortcomings and to allow His Holy Spirit to give you the peace that "passes all understanding."

"And the peace of God, which passeth all understanding, shall keep your hearts and minds through Christ Jesus" (Philippians 4:7).

3

If There Is a God, Where Is He?

Acquired immunodeficiency syndrome (AIDS) has so much stigma attached to it that society assumes the worst when learning that an individual has the dreaded disease. In my opinion, this disease is far worse than the ravages of cancer. Symptoms and secondary infections become a way of life when an individual is diagnosed with the AIDS virus. Medical science has come a long way with the treatment and control of the disease, which has maintained a longer longevity than in the past ten years. Lifestyle choices can be risk factors for the infection, but those factors aren't always the cause of this virus. God loves all persons, but He gives us free choice to do what we want with our lives. He continues to love the sinner but not the sin, and through His infinite mercy He will deal accordingly with each sinner.

Dillon

When the referral for hospice was received on our first AIDS patient, the office scrambled to remember all we had been taught about how to provide nursing care for an individual infected with this virus. Many staff members requested not to be assigned to this case because there was such hysteria and misconception about dealing with it. Fear was a major factor, but God's Word, throughout, says, "Fear not." In fact, I have read that this phrase appears approximately 365 times in the Bible—a "fear not" for every day of the year.

God, am I up for the challenge? I prayed silently; I knew in my spirit I would be assigned this case. Immediately, a peace that can only come from God overwhelmed me and made me realize that I was probably the right one to send. I remembered Isaiah 6:8, which says, "Also I heard the Voice of the Lord saying, Whom shall I send, and who will go for us; Then said I, here am I; send me."

Dillon, a thirty-six year-old extremely intelligent man, had chosen a lifestyle that wasn't acceptable to me as a Christian, but he was in need of a nurse who would minister to his physical health, and I hoped an opportunity would present itself to share my love of Christ with him in a nonjudgmental way. This opportunity was one that I delayed for several months, hoping that God wouldn't lay the burden on my heart to discuss the topic of Dillon's salvation. Don't ever fool yourself into thinking that God won't use every available opportunity to share His love for all creation.

After ignoring the tugging at my heart for weeks, God used a different tactic. He had the audacity to wake me up at 3:00 a.m. to place Dillon on my heart as He had never done before. I was used to being called out frequently during the night for patients but not by a call from God. I wrestled with my spirit, attempting to go back to sleep, but sleep would not come. After a restless night, I arose and said to God, "All right, I will do it, but you must put the words on my lips that need to be said."

I certainly was capable of taking care of Dillon's multiple physical problems, but God was asking a lot from me to manage his spiritual ones as well. Luke 12:12 says, "For the Holy Spirit shall teach you in the same hour what ye ought to say." I was banking on His promise.

A student nurse was training under me at the time, and when she met me for our rounds that morning, she asked what I intended to do at Dillon's visit. She and I had talked many times about the situation and that I was hesitant to share the gospel with him. "I'm going to take the plunge this morning and see what happens," I said, sharing what had transpired during the night. She could tell by my tone that it was going to be either a short, uneventful visit or a long, gratifying one.

Climbing the stairs, we could hear the conversation Dillon was having with his caregiver. I had hoped that Dillon would be resting or not fully awake so I wouldn't have to share anything this visit, and we could do a quick assessment and leave. I still did not want the conversation about salvation to come up.

God had other plans. Sitting on the side of the bed, Dillon was smoking a cigarette and appeared coherent. Many days, he would be confused and wouldn't respond well to conversation. On one occasion, he attempted to light the end of his nose, thinking it was a cigarette. AIDS often causes encephalitis in the meninges

21

of the brain, which was another complication that Dillon was experiencing in the advanced stage of his illness. The encephalitis caused hallucinations, and Dillon would see darkened shadows on the walls, as well as spiders or snakes in his bed or in his room. I felt fairly confident that these were glimpses of what he would experience if he left this world without coming to a saving grace through Christ.

When the nursing assessment was complete, God began pulling at my heartstrings, and I felt the urgency to speak about Him to my young patient, regardless of the outcome. "Dillon," I began very timidly, "do you believe in God?"

There was a long pause before he answered. "No, I don't believe in God or in heaven or hell!"

My heart dropped. *What now, God?* I persevered a little more. "What do you think happens to your body after you die?"

Again, he answered quickly and a little sterner. "Nothing happens; you just die and that is all there is to it." He hadn't asked me to leave yet, but fear was starting to enter in because I was stepping up to risky boundaries.

"God give me some more boldness," I whispered. An inner voice seemed to say, *"Try one more time."* I began to share what had helped me through many obstacles in my life, and I shared the events of my parents' deaths and what they had allowed me to see through their dying experiences. These events didn't betray any privacy issues because they were my own experiences.

Dillon lay back on his bed and turned his back to me, relaying that this conversation was over. Sadly, I left the room feeling that Dillon did not want what God had to offer him. Little did I know that his significant other, Barry, had heard the conversation from the other room. He began to question me about what I had said to Dillon and seemed open to the real evidence of a heaven and a hell. He began to share how much he loved Dillon and that he had been his only partner, but that Dillon had contracted the AIDS virus from another male partner. This conversation wasn't going as I had planned, but at least I learned about the past of this relationship.

I shared what the gospel said about homosexuality and that I was grateful that he hadn't displayed any homosexuality tendencies in my presence, as well as that he had respected my Christian beliefs on this issue. Barry admitted that he had read the Bible and had treated it as just another interesting book to read and then put it on the shelf. I became bolder and explained how this "book" had stood the test of time. The Old Testament prophecies and predictions were written thousands of years before the New Testament by different authors but they relayed the same information through Christ.

Barry, an extremely intelligent man, wanted to know specific Scriptures about homosexuality.

Please help me, Lord. Remember, you wanted me to start this conversation. I was unsure, but I quoted Leviticus 20:13. "If a man also lie with mankind as he lieth with a woman, both of them have committed an abomination; they shall surely be put to death; their blood shall be upon them."

"That is Old Testament Scripture," I said quickly, "but it is found in Romans. Paul certified that homosexuality was a rebellion against the law of God."

Certain that I would be reported to my supervisor and that I would not be wanted at any future visits, Barry politely said,

"Thanks. Enjoyed the conversation. See you next visit, unless I need to page you sooner."

Surprised and not sure if any of my words fell on open ears or an open heart, I excused myself and left.

Sad to say, Dillon's condition rapidly deteriorated, and he became more incoherent daily. The opportunity to discuss his salvation never presented itself again. Had he digested any of our conversation when he'd had that coherent day? Only God knows. But the night of his passing, Barry called and asked me to visit—all the signs I had taught him to look for in the dying process were beginning to happen, and he wanted reassurance that he was doing all he could to help make Dillon comfortable. By the time I arrived, Dillon had died, but Barry relayed that the passing had been easy. "I kept telling him to go to the light as he was dying." This is the only detail that was somewhat comforting to me.

Had Barry shared our conversation with Dillon? The only satisfaction in this story was that I had obeyed what God wanted me to do and had planted a seed so He could do the rest. Is Dillon at peace? I pray that he is. There is nothing too hard for God. I know that early one morning, the Lord woke me up and felt it was important that I share the gospel with Dillon and Barry. The rest was up to Him. Jeremiah 32:27 states, "Behold, I am the Lord, the God of all flesh; is there anything too hard for me?" I am so glad that He is the God of mercy and the God of judgment, not humankind.

Encephalitis, secondary to the AIDS virus, affects the brain, causing erratic, unpredictable behavior and dementia symptoms. Although dementia patients may appear to already have passed on mentally, families and caregivers must listen closely, as coherency can occur through their actions, phrases, singing, or occasional "acting out" behavior. It may seem insignificant but it takes on a whole new meaning if you listen to what is being said. These same behaviors often give caregivers an insight into what is waiting for those dementia patients when they die.

Miss Patty

Patty was a ninety-six-year-old patient suffering from multiple health problems related to her long history of alcohol abuse, as well as the diagnosis of vascular dementia. When Miss Patty was good, she was very, very good, but when she was bad, she was very, very bad. For a small-framed, eighty-six-pound lady (when "soaking wet"), she had arms and legs like an octopus and could fight like a sailor while biting and scratching at the same time. She was never at a loss for words, and at times, those words could shock even the most profane among us.

On a good day, Patty had the sweetest demeanor and moments of such clarity that it was difficult to envision she could go into rages that would physically injury those attempting to do her care. One day when the clarity and coherency were present, I asked her about her faith and asked her to share what she had experienced as a child. I was amazed to find that she had helped to raise her grandsons and had gone to church frequently but did not ever ascribe to a faith in God.

How does one go to church and never have a faith in God? I wondered. Apparently many can do this without following Christ and experiencing His grace in the truest sense, even while being active in a church. Had Miss Patty gone to worship to appease her neighbors or fulfill the expectations of others?

She soon lost interest in my conversation about Jesus, how He forgives, and how He remembers the sin no more. Praying that an opportunity would present itself again, I hurriedly left to continue my day.

Alcohol had become Patty's god, the god she depended on for all of her adult life. A minister would visit her frequently, and on one occasion, I was privy to one of those conversations—I heard a watered-downed sharing of the gospel to a lady who was looking at death directly in the eyes. Where was the bold sharing of God's Word for Patty, letting her know that if she didn't give her heart to Christ, she would be going to hell? Hell seems to be a topic that many ministers don't always feel comfortable discussing with the terminally ill person, particularly if that terminal patient is elderly. Emotions can cloud the mind that this is a "sweet little old lady" whom God could not possibly send to hell. Sadly, I knew He would do so if her heart was not right.

It was the family's or the clergy's responsibility to point this out to her, not mine. I knew as soon as that thought entered into my mind, however, that I was wrong. It is every Christian's duty to love and relay the gospel of Jesus Christ.

As Patty grew frailer and her coherency became less and less, she screamed that she was on fire and to get the spiders and snakes off her. She would scream, "It's hot! It's hot! Get me out, please." The caregiver would attempt to calm her down, but the anxiety would become more intense until she had to be medicated. I often thought, *Was she seeing her final destination?* After I discussed Patty's behavior with her social worker, who then notified her minister, the minister would visit over and over again but never appeared to relieve the hallucinations of fire. Many times, her caregiver shrugged it off, assuming Patty was going through DTs (detoxification related to her history of alcohol abuse), but I knew this wasn't the case. It had been a long time since she had requested any alcohol. Self-detoxification passes within a few days of discontinuing alcohol use. The hunger for the addiction remains, but the detoxification process lingers only a short time.

I vowed to attempt to talk with Miss Patty one more time at my next visit, and I readied myself for the task. As I walked into Miss Patty's home early one morning, it became apparent that she wasn't in her usual place. When I asked where she was, I was informed that she had died the evening before; her family had been alongside her. The on-call nurse hadn't been notified. My first question, as the nurse who had worked with the dying for many years, was if she had a peaceful death. I was sadly informed that it had been a difficult one and that she struggled a great deal, despite having pain medication. I knew in my spirit that it had not been a physical pain but a spiritual one that caused the struggled passing.

God is a merciful and a just God, but I was left with an unrest that more should have been done for Miss Patty. I know that we have free will and are allowed to make our own choice to follow Jesus or not to follow His path, but my inner peace isn't there whenever I remember Miss Patty.

As Christians, missed opportunities will haunt us if an opportunity arises to discuss Christ with a person, and we don't follow that small inward voice and respond to His leading. We may not get the effect that we might hope for when discussing the gospel, but an inner peace will always fill our spirits when at least we try.

Miss Patty was an opportunity that did not turn out to be the positive outcome that I had prayed for, and I knew I hadn't relied on the Holy Spirit to guide me in that endeavor, as God had expected of me. I pray that the Lord nurtured that nugget that was planted in Patty years ago and that she has entered into a place of rest.

Martin

God will bring avenues to a Christian, no matter what career or job one may have, in order to share His gospel with others ... which brings me to Martin.

Martin was a hard man who had been a coal miner since he was very young. He also was a very abusive man to his wife and family and had been for many years. Ordinarily, I never would have crossed paths with Martin, as I was the director of hospice at the time, but one of my staff had an accident and would be off for several weeks, which necessitated my picking up her workload.

Every Christian who is into God's Word knows that nothing evil comes from our Father, but He sometimes allows certain things to happen to create an avenue for something greater to happen in His name. My colleague's accident wasn't of God, but through that accident, I got to meet Martin.

I had heard stories about this man before I ever made my first visit. The stories weren't reassuring to me; in fact, they were quite intimidating and daunting. He never wanted anyone to visit from our agency; he just wanted to be left alone, but finally he agreed when his spouse said she couldn't do his care any longer. Most of the time he just wanted a nurse to check him and "get out." He refused to move or participate in making it easier for the caregiver to turn or reposition him. He constantly complained that he needed something for his pain, and if we weren't going to do that, "Then get out." This became his usual conversation. The years of alcohol abuse required that he be medicated for the withdrawal and necessitated strong observation of the narcotic usage.

During my drive to see Martin, I prayed frequently that God would let me be a positive influence on him and not an irritation. He had become used to his routine visiting nurse, who had developed a somewhat passive relationship with him; now he would be introduced to a different person who would ask more questions to become familiar with his case.

Betty, a very small, stoop-shouldered woman, greeted me at the door with downcast eyes. In a voice that was almost whisper, she invited me into the living room, where her husband, Martin, now confined to the hospital bed, lay with his eyes closed and his mouth clenched tightly shut. It was apparent by his body language that I needed to be prepared for a battle of wits.

"Good morning, Martin," I said and then smiled at his son, who was sitting close to his Dad's side.

Martin responded with harsh, angry words. "What do you want? Where is that other nurse who usually comes? Why can't you just leave me alone?"

Very purposefully, I answered each of his questions with a smile, despite feeling butterflies and just wanting to run out the door. God would give me the strength to face any task that was put before me. Martin needed me, even though he hadn't come to realize it yet. Grudgingly, he allowed me to do an assessment of his pain and condition.

I saw a picture on the hearth of him as a soldier. I soon realized that Martin had been a veteran in World War II, a war that my father had participated in also. I hoped this was to be my connection to him. All through my physical assessment, I mentioned things about my Dad and the kind of man he had become, despite the atrocities he had seen in battle. Soon, I noticed that Martin was not swearing when I asked him to take a deep breath or if it hurt when I pressed a certain spot.

I left that initial visit with ambivalent feelings for having used my wonderful dad, who had passed on several years before, as a means to get Martin to open up to me. It was as if I could hear my dad's words softly whispering in my ear: *"Babe, keep on using me. This is the seed faith that you learned from me many years ago."* Such peace and thankfulness came over me in knowing that I had had a special Christian dad. The young man sitting by his dad in that house I'd recently left hadn't been so fortunate, but Martin still had that chance to be a kind of dad to his son before he had to cross over.

Now I knew why God had put me in this place and time. I had to work fast before it was too late for Martin. He needed what my dad had experienced in his walk with Christ, and now I had the means with the Holy Spirit to do just that. "God give me time to do this. Don't take him from his family until I at least have shared Your gospel with him," I prayed.

I visited Martin three times a week, and at each visit, I noticed he talked more and cursed less. He liked talking about his job as a coal miner and occasionally would share an event that happened while he served in the military. His son always waited by his bedside and appeared to hang on every word his dad said, as a man in the desert would thirst for water. Were these the only times Martin ever really talked to his family without some form of ridicule or physical abuse? "God, continue to soften his heart, and give me time and opportunity to share Your saving grace"—this became my prayer before each visit.

One particular visit would be different because I knew Martin's crossing-over journey was about to begin, and I needed to tell him about Jesus before it was too late. I knew Martin was deteriorating physically, and he needed more medication to keep him comfortable, but with each increase of the narcotic, he would become drowsier and less talkative. I was running out of quality time.

After completing my assessment, I asked Martin if I could ask him a very personal question and, miraculously, he said yes. Before I lost my nerve, I asked, "Martin if you were to die today, do you know where your spirit would go?"

Seconds passed, which seemed like an eternity, before he responded. I braced myself for the string of expletives that I expected would come from his mouth, but God is alive and still in control. He had softened Martin's heart.

Martin finally answered, "I know I am bound for hell. I have abused my body and abused my relationships with my wife and son." Instead of his cursing, tears of regret streamed down his face for a life wasted through alcohol and reckless living.

Still a little uncomfortable about my relationship with him, I asked. "Do you want me to pray with you? Or would you like a minister to visit?"

"I feel I need to share several things with a minister," he said. "Things that have led me to this point in this life."

I phoned a local minister and stressed how important that it was that he visit as soon as possible. He assured me he would visit that same evening. I had an uncomfortable feeling about that assurance, though, as I had been misled by clergy many times in the past. Still, I had to trust in God's leading for this promise.

Not able to wait until Martin's scheduled visit two days later, I decided to visit the next day. Immediately when I entered the room, I sensed a change. I could feel God's presence, and a peacefulness that wasn't there before had softened Martin's face. The son was holding his dad's hand, and Martin's wife was smiling as she attempted to feed him. Motioning for me to come closer, Martin's voice, now barely a whisper, spoke so clearly to me about a dream he'd had the night before.

After the minister had visited, and Martin gave his heart to Jesus, he'd slept without pain. He awoke sometime during the night and saw angels on the winding staircase in the living room that led upstairs. Those angels were motioning for him to come on up. He could hear their music and saw such beauty from the light. He couldn't contain his joy.

God had softened his heart. God had used an unworthy vessel like me; I'd used an avenue prepared for me a long time ago by my earthly dad, the "seed planter," to bring a hard-core man—who easily could have been dismissed as not important—to the saving grace of Jesus Christ. Everyone is important to God, and relationships can be mended with the working of the Holy Spirit.

Martin was given only a few more weeks of a physical life, but that time before he crossed over to his eternal life was spent sharing with his son and wife about God's infinite love. Harsh words and a lifetime of physical abuse were wiped clean, and his family was given a glimpse of how God can take the most evil characteristics of humankind and make a new creation through His Son, Jesus Christ.

I'd heard it said that an angel sings whenever a saint is called home. Certainly, the angels that God allowed Martin to see on his staircase were rejoicing that another saint would be coming home, never to experience pain and suffering from the Evil One again.

Thank you, God, for allowing me to be blessed by the change in Martin. My faith is stronger for the encounter that was put before me. A door opened to me that I hesitantly walked through, with Christ leading the way.

"With men it is impossible, but not with God; for with God all things are possible" (Mark 10:27).

4

Why Me, God?

God will put you in places where the Evil One is working to see if your faith can stand up to the test. My faith has always been steady, and Christ has always been a priority in my life. I knew God had led me to the nursing career I had chosen a long time before I met Abigail. Never in my nursing, to this point, had my faith been questioned as to whether I was serving God or Satan.

The question "Why me, God?" became the resounding theme while working with the next family. Why had God put me in a situation to be trampled on, emotionally and spiritually? Wasn't I doing a good job of following His leading? Didn't I tackle family dynamics better than most of my colleagues?

Prideful people can be brought to their knees when they start to depend on themselves rather than depending on God. So why me, God? Very soon, this seasoned nurse was to learn a great lesson from the "school of hard knocks."

Abigail

One of the darkest moments of my career was when I was dealing with middle-aged Abigail and her family. Abigail had been told at her last doctor's appointment that her cancer wasn't responding to the treatments and had spread throughout her body. She chose to come home and be comfortable with hospice care for whatever time she had left to live.

To hospice nurses, family dynamics can be more of a challenge at times than the difficult work with the terminal patient. Family dynamics are never predictable; the goals and relationships with the loved one who has a terminal prognosis can bring out the best—or the worst—in members of that family. Emotional guilt of the past, anxiety about the impending death, betrayal of neglecting the relationship, not being home enough, or anger at God for allowing this to happen may become very prominent when there aren't past healthy relationships to draw upon. Members begin to pull in different directions without being focused on an outcome that the loved one has chosen. It becomes self-focused.

The dynamics of this family were like none I had encountered before and have not encountered since. They had different goals in mind than Abigail had. Their goals were that God would heal her completely in her physical life and that their prayers and avoidance of dealing with the what-ifs weren't to be discussed, not in front of Abigail or any of the family members.

As a palliative care nurse, I preferred to have a social worker present at the time of an admission to deal with any out-of-control family dynamics that might occur. Today was no different; my insightful social worker was by my side. After entering Abigail's home, something in my spirit made me feel as if this wouldn't go well—a circle of family members surrounded Abigail in an almost defiant manner and certainly a protective one.

When introductions were completed, I started to explain why hospice had been called due to the recent outcome of the last physician's visit and Abigail's terminal prognosis. Immediately, the daughter's hand went up to stop the conversation because she felt it was moving in a negative way and that only praise and positive words were to be spoken in this house.

The social worker looked to me, and we both looked to Abigail for some confirmation of what she wanted. Abigail sat quietly, very demure, not expressing any emotions. Each question we asked, hoping she would answer, was immediately stopped by a family member relaying his or her opinion. In all my years of nursing and with numerous difficulties I had been experienced with family dynamics, this was the first time that words failed me. The social worker also was at a loss for words. I could not understand why we had been asked to come. We had called to verify the date and time for the admission. Why hadn't they told us then about their objections to hospice?

Despite numerous attempts to discuss the hospice program and the goals for comfort and pain control, we were countered with someone telling us, "God will take care of this in His healing plan." One remark cut deep into my spirit—I was accused of doing evil and of working for the Devil because I was talking about death and dying. This was the first time my faith had been questioned by someone who didn't know my years of walking with God.

I have been blessed to see God's healing come in many forms to many individuals throughout my years of nursing. I know healing always comes from our heavenly Father and can come in an earthly healing or in the spiritual form by passing from this life to life eternal. In my mind came the words from a godly woman and minister's wife who had passed from this life to her eternal reward. She knew I would grieve her passing when God called her home. Her words will always remain in my heart and mind: "If everyone is healed in this life, no one would ever die." I wanted to let these words pass from my lips to Abigail's family, but Psalm 51:10 took over in my spirit. "Create in me a clean heart, O God and renew a right spirit within me."

In order for me to have that right spirit, I had to keep quiet and take the accusations and the hurtful words, just as Christ once had to endure. But one thing I could do was to end the conversation so they could think it over and decide if they wanted hospice's help in the future. They would have to make the call for our return.

That call came a few days later from Abigail herself. She wanted what our team had to offer her through the hospice program. With a great deal of trepidation, I returned to the home but was pleasantly surprised to find Abigail alone and very eager to talk. She knew that God was going to call her home shortly; she just couldn't get her family to understand that God was going to heal her through death. What a wonderful visit we had that day, and we looked forward to future days of sharing our faith in Christ and what was in store for her, That, however, was not to be. The family returned, and the accusations and hurtful remarks started again. It got to be so difficult that doing a physical assessment of Abigail's comfort was almost impossible.

"God will take care of her pain. He will take care of her bowels and will take care of her appetite," a family member said. She had become the caregiver, and everything had to go through her. She requested that another nurse be sent since I insisted on asking questions about Abigail's health.

This tore at my heart. Abigail and I had had several weeks of beautiful conversations about the Lord and His divine healing. Apparently, I couldn't say the right things to her children, and when I did say anything, it was misconstrued as being of the Devil.

As the director of hospice, it was easy for me to assign another nurse to Abigail—one I knew was about the same age as her children and who would be able to share memories of their childhoods. This nurse assessed but never asked how Abigail was doing because she knew of my encounter with this family.

At staff meetings, we would share that we felt sad that Abigail wasn't allowed to have the peaceful outcome that we had hoped for her, the outcome she deserved. Clergy was brought in, but he too was rebuffed because he attempted to discuss dying with the family.

Forgiveness comes so much easier than forgetfulness. At this point in my career, I began to question if I was doing God's plan to which He had led me so many years ago. I almost gave up nursing, even though I had yearned for and worked so hard to achieve it. Praying to God to send me a message of what He wanted me to do became harder and harder because those doubts kept entering my mind from the Evil One. Maybe talking about death and dying *wasn't* from God.

One night, about a month after Abigail's death, I was suddenly awakened and was overwhelmed with a sense of peace. God's words came clearly to me that He never leaves us or forsakes us. He was with me all along. Beautiful memorials began to flood my mind of all the lives I had touched in my nursing. In their dying, I had blessed them and brought them to the saving knowledge of Christ. In the midst of sharing about God, and yes, in the midst of sharing about death, many had been blessed. I wasn't going to let this experience ruin my faith and lessen the chance of bringing others to God's peace before they died. I immediately felt my bruised heart begin to heal.

Had pride been in my thoughts of what a good nurse I was? Had pride shut a doorway in my heart to the Holy Spirit because I hadn't asked for advice in dealing with this patient and her family? God had equipped me with His Word to deal with the hurtful remarks and with the reasoning behind the actions of this family, but I hadn't asked for His help. I continued to lick my wounds and make it all about "Why me, God?" and not "Why not me, God?"

After that trial, many asked me to visit and to pray for those dying without direction. God had carried me through that valley, even though I didn't know He was doing it at the time. Thank you, Lord, for Your strength in good times and in bad times. That dark valley made me stronger and more self-assured in my faith; that family failed at their attempts to bring my faith into question.

"God is our refuge and strength, a very present help in trouble" (Psalm 46:1).

Kathleen

Marriage is ordained by God, and throughout that union He must be in every aspect of the relationship. Added stressors can arise when one spouse is an only child. More important, when the husband is the "only son," the harmony of the relationship may be disrupted. This was the case for me.

My husband was the only child with whom his parents were blessed, as his mother had ovarian cancer after his birth that required a total hysterectomy. He was the most important person in her life, and she doted on him, catering to his every whim, doing without to see that he was educated and could become the electrical engineer that he desired to be, and making sure he went to church and walked with God during his life while at home and away at college.

When we decided to get married, he was hesitant to share the news with his mother for many months, claiming she would have difficulty getting used to the idea that he would not be dependent on her. We hadn't been married long before I found out how right he was about another female taking his mother's "place." I had to learn how to wash his clothes the right way, cook his meals the right way, and clean our home the right way.

I was raised to be independent and already had my own routine for the tasks at home, as I had been in the workforce since graduating from high school. I was now twenty-three years old; I didn't need the guidance she was offering.

During the first seven years of our marriage, most disagreements centered on something his mother had said or had done. Newly married couples like their privacy and independence, but we had moved into an apartment next to my husband's parents. Throughout those years, two things remained constant: his mother loved the Lord, and she loved her son.

"God, I found my soul mate, so why does his mother have to be part of that equation?" I would often ask after yet another disagreement. I grew up in a household where love was shown to all who entered our home. My parents enveloped my new husband with love and kindness without showing any bias.

Sometimes we can forget who is in control of all situations—the One who is just waiting to be asked to help sort out problems and resolve the conflicts. That is Jesus Christ through His Holy Spirit. Many times in the past I had called upon His name for help. Why had I failed to do so in this season of my life?

Turning to God's Word, I prayed that the Lord would take this anger from me and deal with my heart so that I could grow to love this woman as Ruth of the Bible loved her mother-in-law, Naomi.

"So that we may boldly say, the Lord is my Helper and I will not fear what man (or woman) shall do unto me" (Hebrews 13:6). This verse was to become a vital Scripture throughout the years ahead, giving me strength and encouragement.

I wish I could say that the next thirty-three years were smooth sailing, but I can say that the storms became fewer and the love grew stronger between my mother-in-law and me. God tempered both our hearts and allowed us to share a common bond for a wonderful man that we both loved and respected.

My father-in-law, whom I loved completely and without hesitation from the first time we met, had died four years earlier, leaving a vast void in all of our lives. I remember one of our last conversations as clearly as if were only days ago instead of years; it concerned my mother-in-law, Kathleen. He told me he knew it had been difficult for me over the years, being a daughter-in-law to his wife, but he knew that in her own way she had grown to love and respect me. He said that he soon would be going home (he had metastatic lung cancer) and only had a short time to be with us. He had a heavenly home waiting for him, but he had one request to make of me.

In my heart, I knew what he was going to say. *Why me, God?* I thought. *Don't let him ask me what I think he is going to ask.*

But he asked it anyway. Looking directly into my eyes, he pleaded, "Please look out for Kathleen for me. She is going to need you now more than ever." This patient, kind, Christian man was asking a lot from me, but out of love and respect for him, I answered him without hesitation: "With God's help, I will do my best."

Little did I know that I would have to keep this promise that I made to my father-in-law so soon. The years started to take their toll on Kathleen, and the independent lady, now in her eighties, had to depend on us for help with even the menial tasks of daily living. After she sustained multiple fractures from falls, due to her rambling around in the very large old home where my husband was raised, plans had to be made about what to do for her health and well-being.

Her body was failing, but her mind was still very sharp. She had always wanted to have a smaller home in her early years of her marriage, but that dream never came to fruition. Now might be the time to fulfill that for her, but I knew it would require a monetary sacrifice on our part. *God, why me? I promised to help care for her, but this may be going too far—dipping into our savings for a home for her.* Then I immediately felt ashamed of my selfishness because Christ had sacrificed it all for me, spilled His blood for me, and ultimately died on a cross for me. This was money that really belonged to God in the first place, and what better way to demonstrate His love for others than to use it unselfishly. We purchased land and built her a home directly across the street from us. God made the way because that land wouldn't have been up for sale otherwise.

After this decision was made, I thanked God for that plan because as her health began to fail, she was just across the street in a small, handicapped-accessible home, where we could help meet her needs as they arose. In all the years of our marriage, I never heard any words of thankfulness from her, but many neighbors and our church family said she would often talk about how fortunate she was to have a daughter-in-law to care for her in such a loving way. It must have been difficult for her to share her feelings with me. I wondered if I made it difficult for her or if it was the way she had been raised.

I prepared my husband for his mother's passing after I'd seen the signs for several weeks prior to that crossing over. There became a silent truce between us, and such respect grew out of this truce that it had to be from God. I washed and cleaned her as if she was my own mother, sharing words of kindness when it was appropriate, ministering to her spiritual needs as she expected.

Her Bible was worn from use, and when I reached for it to read, I found pictures and clippings sandwiched between the pages: clippings of our wedding, pictures of her granddaughter and great-grandchildren, and—much to my surprise—clippings about my accomplishments at college and from my work. She couldn't say well done to me audibly, but God was showing me now, silently, how she felt. Everything that was important to her had been stuffed between the pages of God's Word.

Christmas Eve 2005 was to be etched in my family's minds for a long time. Bed-bound now and drifting slowly into a state of drowsy euphoria, Kathleen would smile as she heard the great-grandchildren laughing and playing in the living room. Many times, they made pictures and put them on the dresser for her to see. She would kiss them as she was able and then drift off to sleep.

Christmas morning arrived, and the rest of the family were preparing for church. I shared with her that it was Christmas. I wasn't sure if she heard me, but she opened her eyes long enough to say, "Happy birthday, Jesus." Then, turning her head toward me, she stated very sternly, "If I die on Christmas, I can't help it."

Where had that come from? *God, don't let her mean spirit stay. I rebuke it in the name of Jesus.* It didn't appear again. God wasn't about to let Satan undo the healing that had occurred between us over the past few years.

Christmas Day passed quickly. Kathleen drifted into a coma early the next day. Her breathing became very shallow, almost difficult to see because she had such a peaceful demeanor about her. She had no difficulty breathing, no audible secretions, and no restlessness that I knew dying patients often experienced. *Thank you, God, for sparing her and our family from these difficult signs in the dying process.* As her breaths became farther and farther apart, I knew God was letting her cross over, and now was the time for last words to her.

God allows wonderful things to happen during this transition to demonstrate that things are going to be all right and that loved ones often reach out in some way to those being left behind. My mother-in-law's eyes opened wide, which had not happened for many hours, and her head turned toward the son she loved so much and gazed lovingly at him. The most beautiful words came from my husband to his dying mother, which will always humble my spirit. He said with a breaking heart, "I love you, Mom. Go on."

She immediately closed her eyes and went to her place of rest. Her only son had given her permission to transition to the other side, just as God's Son had been given permission to transition to His Father when He said, "It is finished."

That question of "Why me, God?" proved to be such a wonderful experience that if it hadn't been me, I would have missed the blessing of a godly woman who touched my life through a son who was been raised to respect and love the women in his life. He continues to be a loving husband, dad, and grandfather, thanks to the training from God's Word and discipline from two very godly parents.

Mother, Present with the Lord

My mother died October 6, 1988, at the age of sixty-nine, from a long battle with non-Hodgkin's lymphoma; it invaded all of the lymphatic systems of her body. During those three years of the disease process, many Christians brought her books on faith healing, and many times they said very hurtful things to her: "Your faith must not be strong enough, or God would heal you," and "You must be paying for some sin in your life."

Attacking her faith was so destructive to her that she too began to question "why me?" I believe that illness and disease come from the Evil One, not from our heavenly Father, but God allows things to happen to strengthen others' faith, or He has a larger plan to heal them in the spiritual sense, not always in the physical realm.

After Mother's death, some of those hurtful words came back to my memory, flooding me with discomfort and doubts. The mother I knew and loved had brought me up in a Christian home and demonstrated love for Christ in all of her actions, but now I needed to know if she was present with the Lord.

God always reveals His truth in some form if you ask in faith. He always brings the peace that you yearn for and need. He didn't fail me in my quest for truth once again.

The day before the funeral, I was resting on the bed, not certain, even to this day, if I was asleep or awake, but Mother's face appeared before me in such radiance that it filled the room with light. Without words but with an understanding, she conveyed to me, with a smile of peace and serenity, "I am all right. Don't you worry anymore. It's all love and peace here." That was the only time I was allowed to have such a vision of Mother.

I felt comfortable enough to share this vision with only a few people—my husband, Mother's youngest sister, and my minister at the time. Sharing with these trustworthy individuals strengthened my faith that healing does often come in a spiritual way through death. My pastor said, "God does show the faithful what they are hungering to know. Frequently that knowledge can come by a dream or a vision."

Several weeks later, I learned that Mother's sister had a dream in which she saw the same radiant face and body but fully clothed in a magenta-colored dress (which was Mother's favorite), and she conveyed the same message to her.

My nagging doubts dissipated after that, and I knew God had eased my mind that Mother was safely in His presence by allowing me a glimpse of her reward of faith. How I wanted to share this experience with those who said such hurtful words during her disease process, but the peace that I had from this vision was too private to share with those who were so narrow-minded about God and what He can do. After this, I vowed never to express those same hurtful words to the dying. I would allow God to direct my words and actions through the Holy Spirit. I would pray with my patients for healing and allow God to choose what method He was going to use. God always heals!

"And I say unto you, Ask and it shall be given you; seek and ye shall find; knock and it shall be opened unto you" (Luke 11: 9).

God had opened a door for me to ease my pain, which blessed and humbled my spirit about how much He cared for me and affirmed that He should never be put in a box. God is ready to ease whatever burden the faithful have on their hearts. All we need to do is ask.

"Take my yoke upon you, and learn of me; for I am meek and lowly in heart; and ye shall find rest unto your souls. For my yoke is easy and my burden is light" (Matthew 11:29–30).

5

Better Look, Listen, and Feel, or You'll Miss the Blessing

I am a firm believer that God speaks and shows the dying what He has in store for them, and through that sharing, loved ones and families, in their grief, can be blessed if they truly listen and pay attention to what is happening in the dying process. At this point, doubters may be thinking that most people aren't able to share during the final phase of their dying. I beg to differ! The following incidents may cause doubters to reevaluate this misconception.

Fred and the Clock That Wouldn't Chime

I was privileged to get to know an extremely close-knit family that viewed death as a simple passing from this life to the next life. Fred and his wife had shared many hardships during their marriage that many would never have to experience. The loss of their only son to a violent act only deepened their commitment to each other and to their other children. Fred was the patriarch of this family, to whom all had looked for guidance and support. Rarely did one see Fred without his beautiful wife of forty-eight years, Sharon.

Fred and Sharon loved to smoke. They realized the hazards, but like so many others, they thought they would never develop the dreaded lung cancer. Fred wasn't so fortunate; after years of heavy smoking, he was diagnosed with terminal lung cancer, which, when found, had metastasized to the bone. On the day of the admission to hospice care, I was welcomed by a warm and realistic family.

Their goal was that Fred should be comfortable and surrounded by his family during the final weeks. When questioned about their faith, they assured me they were a strong Catholic family who attended mass weekly. They believed that there was paradise and hell, where you get your rewards. Their priest visited frequently. "That is all taken care of," Sharon stated.

During the final weeks of Fred's life, I saw such love and caring given to him. They had a schedule so that a family member would always be present to assist in whatever capacity was needed. It was so heartwarming for me to work with their family dynamics. Often, this wasn't the case. Many times in other families, quarrels and blaming games would raise their ugly heads and cause increased stress on the dying. Death should be a time of bonding and healing, not a time of tearing apart.

Fred's priest came without being called by any of the hospice staff. When I knew that Fred was actively dying, the priest performed the last rites, which seemed to be a comfort to the family. By this time, Fred was comatose, and his eyes remained closed during the last two days of his life. A family member never left the bedside and was always willing to help turn and reposition him, as well as assist with the terminal care that was done at this point.

When I realized that Fred imminently would die, I asked if the family wanted to be present. To my surprise, the room became surrounded by siblings and grandchildren, all showing their grief in tears and expressing how much Fred would be missed.

Sharon was sitting on the bed, holding his hand, when Fred opened his eyes, turned toward his beautiful wife of so many years, and—with a smile but no words—took his last breath to cross over to his reward. What astonished everyone present, however, was that their anniversary clock in the living room, which hadn't chimed in many years, chimed one time as Fred took that final breath in his earthly body. What a beautiful memory God allowed this family to share and a reminder of the love God has for His faithful children and the type of love He wants between marriage partners. I have read in God's Word that the angels rejoice at the faithful coming home.

Did an angel ring that anniversary clock to let the family know that Fred was coming home? Had this family not been present, they wouldn't have experienced the blessing that was in store for them. They looked, listened, and felt the blessing God showed them in Fred's crossing over. I thank God I was present for that blessing.

Cindy

Cindy was a beautiful, petite, soft-spoken young woman who had been born with cystic fibrosis. The exacerbation of the disease was controlled for many years with multiple hospitalizations and medications. When finally the exacerbations became more frequent and the medications became less effective, Cindy was told that she needed to prepare to die. Nothing more could be done for her.

I was fortunate to have Cindy as a patient for many years in home care prior to the admission into hospice. She and I had become friends, and she confided in me a great deal about what was going to happen to her. We shared about God and about her heavenly home that was waiting for her at the end of her earthly journey. Cindy had been raised in a religious home, but Christian was in name only. She prayed to change her mother's outlook on faith and her husband's vow that he did not want any part of religion.

Whenever her spouse, Timmy, entered the room, she would immediately stop asking questions about Christ or His Word. I would continue sharing as I did her care, hoping that Timmy would grasp a seed of faith. He was comfortable with me and always preferred that I visit rather than any of the other staff, which helped me to be bold in my conversations. I knew he loved Cindy very much and couldn't fathom life without her. He had done excellent care for her throughout their years of marriage.

On many days, the shortness of breath became so violent that she wasn't able to carry on conversation and could manage only a weak smile. Timmy would become more withdrawn and angry at God for allowing this to happen. Denial and anger becomes a way of coping for many people—an escape from having to deal with the reality of being left alone. Timmy became more anxious as the disease progressed and decided that he wouldn't be able to keep Cindy at home until her death, as she desired. This caused more anger at God and the blame game began. "If there truly is a God, why would He let her suffer like this?" he barked out when he was told that it was time for hospital or home. "If that's the kind of God He is, I don't want any part of Him!"

I quietly told him that Jesus didn't spare His own Son, that He suffered and died for us so that we may have eternal life, but the words appeared to fall on deaf ears. Timmy wasn't ready to listen or to let go of the woman he loved so dearly.

In the hospital, Timmy camped out at her bedside, only leaving long enough to get something to eat. He still felt that she would get better one more time, despite the doctors and nurses informing him otherwise. He didn't pray for a divine healing; his faith was strictly in the health care professionals and medications. I attempted to again ask for a minister to pray or to allow me to pray, but he became angry and emphatically said, "No!"

By this time, Cindy was semi-comatose and restless—a restlessness I knew she had about leaving her family. She had been bed-bound since admission to the facility and was oxygen-dependent, but her small body continued to struggle with each breath. She occasionally mumbled words that were incoherent, but she also uttered in almost a whisper, "I want to go home." Timmy would cry and say, "I'm sorry, but I can't take you home until you're better." And her restlessness would increase.

As a seasoned palliative care nurse, I recognized what was happening with Cindy and what she was trying to convey to her husband and mother. She was asking for their permission to go to her heavenly home and to be rid of the ravaged body in which she had been trapped for so many years. When I shared my belief of this, Timmy refused to listen and refused to give her the permission to go on. He couldn't grant that request because he was adamant that she was asking to go back to their small home to see that little dog she loved so desperately.

Also, as an end-of-life care nurse I have to know when to back away and allow God to take control. Soon, that happened. Without waiting any longer for Timmy or her mother to grant that request, Cindy raised herself from the bed and stood upright (even though she had been bed-bound for two weeks), smiled, raised her face toward the ceiling, and loudly shouted, "I'm going home now!" Timmy caught her as she began to collapse to the floor, and she died in his arms.

Cindy went home without her earthly family giving her the permission that she desperately was asking for. Even months after her passing, Timmy had guilt feelings about not allowing her to go back to their home to spend her last weeks. I have no way of knowing if he ever truly understood what happened in that hospital room. He sold their small home and moved away. God only knows the answer to that question. Timmy was looking, listening, and feeling but wasn't understanding what Cindy was sharing with him at her passing. He was so blocked in grief that he missed the blessing that God had opened to him.

Martha—"I Can't Climb the Stairs"

Throughout my work with patients in their final journeys, many touch my heart because they have no family who can or who are willing to share in this critical time. Such was the case with Martha. She had been a hard, domineering, promiscuous woman most of her life, and her children and family no longer wanted to be a part of her life. She was intellectually disabled, which might have accounted for others taking advantage of her sexually. She only had a small apartment and a meager income to sustain her well-being.

To my knowledge, Martha never attended a church and didn't have a strong faith in God. Over the years, her life had taken a toll on her body; she had stomach cancer and diabetes, both lower legs were amputated, and she was wheelchair-bound. She had never learned to walk with any prosthetic devices after her amputations. Her physician had referred her to hospice but sternly stated that we were to keep her home.

One of the regulations of hospice care is that there must be a twenty-four–hour caregiver present during palliative care at home, or the patient does not meet the criteria for admission. Martha did not have a caregiver. This left a terrible dilemma for our agency, but we persevered to find some help. Martha had touched the hearts of many at a local agency that delivered her meals, and they agreed to take turns being the appointed caregiver, with her permission. She gladly agreed and was admitted to the program.

Her palliative care, however, began to take a toll on the hospice staff, as she had multiple symptoms to control, and the caregivers changed so frequently that they couldn't adequately learn about the disease process. Everything became an emergency for the different caregivers. Being on call twenty-four hours took on a new meaning for us—it meant handling most of their problems for them because they had not been properly educated about what was going to happen. This wasn't their fault, but the help they were giving wasn't handled correctly.

Over the years I have learned that when there are multiple caregivers there needs to be a meeting of all involved so everyone is on the same page. A meeting was set and instructions and education was given on Martha's condition. This went very well. One of the points emphasized to the caregivers was that pain comes in different forms—physical, psychosocial, and spiritual. Much of Martha's pain was spiritual. She wasn't ready to meet her Creator because she had not asked for forgiveness from God or from her family. The forgiveness of God would be the easy part; the family might not be so easily accomplished.

Finding her family proved to be very disheartening for the staff—the family no longer wanted to be a part of Martha's last days. As her nurse, this caused only more concern for me, as her many symptoms of distress were of a spiritual nature, and time was running short that these could be resolved. God always proves to the weak that all they need to do is seek, and He will give them the answers or direct their paths with the Holy Spirit. They need to stay focused with their eyes on Him. Many times people try to handle everything by their own doing, which causes frustration. That was what I was doing again. I had stopped looking, listening, and feeling, as I had taught so many times to families.

I began to listen intently for an opportunity to discuss Martha's past with her and tell her that Christ was standing by, just waiting for her to call out His name. I didn't have to wait long. Early one morning, I found Martha distressful and thrashing, about saying, "I see the light, but I can't get up the steps to reach it. I can't walk. Oh, help me, Jesus."

Martha needed the help that only Jesus can give. Gently, I knelt down to talk with Martha and let her know that it was me, as Martha's eyesight was deteriorating due to her brittle diabetes. She immediately grabbed my hand and repeated the same worry to me—that she saw the light but couldn't get to it because she couldn't walk.

I asked, "Do you know what this light might be and why you need help getting to it?" I knew the answer; I just wanted her to verbalize it.

She began to confess the things that she had done in her life. "I know I won't reach the light," she said, meaning Jesus, "because I'm not fit for heaven."

"Martha, do you want me to do the sinner's prayer with you?" I cautiously asked.

Martha could become violent at times, and I didn't want this to be one of those times. She answered, "I'm too embarrassed to talk to you. I want a minister to come."

"Please, God; let me find a clergy who is willing to come while the timing is right." After I said these words, I realized that everything comes in God's time, and He wouldn't fail Martha now. A Holy Spirit-filled minister agreed to come to talk to Martha that evening. From what I knew about him, nothing would be held back to make the way for Martha to be forgiven.

At the visit the next day, I sensed a change in Martha; calmness and peace seemed to surround her bed. It was as if I was walking into the presence of angels who were waiting to take her home. Martha died later that day, and I know that when she saw that light again, she was able to run up those stairs to meet Christ with assurance that God loved and forgave her of all her transgressions.

This is the importance of why, in the presence of the dying, one must look, listen, and feel, or the blessing will be lost.

Over the years, it has been troubling to my spirit when a person is dying, and he or she hasn't found a peace that can only come with the translation by Jesus Christ. And what is even more troubling is when the person requests a minister, but one isn't willing to come unless it is an opportune time for him or her. The crossing over of the terminally ill doesn't come with a time stamp on their foreheads, but a hospice nurse recognizes certain signs and symptoms and realizes that the opportunity to accept Jesus has to be soon; there won't be another opportunity. Most individuals with whom I have worked want a clergy, not a nurse, for that spiritual affirmation before death. Ed was a prime example of the gravity and urgency for a minister's visit.

Ed—the Man Who Had No Time for God

Ed, a long-time alcoholic and a three-packs-a-day cigarette smoker, had never felt God was important in his life. His petite wife shared about her life with him and that despite pleading and praying for her husband's salvation, it didn't happen. Now he was at death's door with a probable destination of hell unless we could reach him today. Today was the key component that would pass very quickly and with it the chance to give his heart to Christ.

This rough individual caroused, worked, and drank, and then the cycle would start all over the next day. Unfortunately, his fate was sealed when Ed was diagnosed with terminal cancer, and he had to have his tongue and larynx surgically removed related to this disease and the choices he had made over the years. Ed was unable to talk and had to be fed nothing but liquids for the months after the surgery. He would use a communication board to convey his wishes and desires. He often would become agitated when he was unable to make himself understood to his family or any health care worker who visited. Then he would motion for everyone to leave the room.

On the last day I visited, Ed was restless and motioning to me about something that was bothering him. I knew immediately what was causing his terminal restlessness. He was lucid but refused to use his communication board. His wife sat in the bedroom, weeping softly and saying she didn't know what to do to make him comfortable. She had been giving him his liquid medication as prescribed, but nothing helped. With calmness that only came from the Holy Spirit, I asked Ed if he knew that his time to cross over was coming soon. "Is there anything I can do to make your transition easier?" I asked and then hurriedly added that I needed to share something with him. He nodded his head, indicating that he knew already what I was going to share. He pointed downward, signifying that his destination was not a good place. I prayed with him and asked if he wanted a minister to visit; he quickly agreed that he did.

The task of finding a willing minister to visit became very daunting and frustrating to me. Every minister I called said that he could not come because Ed didn't attend that minister's church or that he didn't have the time that day. Many said they would probably come the next day—probably! Ed didn't have the next day; he was down to hours or even less if he slipped into a comatose state.

God always supplies the avenue when it is needed, particularly when there is a lost soul to bring into the fold.

He immediately brought a dedicated minister to my mind that I could call, but I knew he worked at one of our local factories and was in the middle of a shift. I called anyway. After informing him of the urgency, he said he would get cleaned up and come right away.

Pastor Brent arrived less than thirty minutes after my call, and as he entered the bedroom, he too realized that time was short for Ed. He led him in the sinner's prayer, and Ed squeezed Pastor's hand in affirmation that he understood. Soon, the restlessness disappeared, and Ed took his last breath an hour later. Thank God for dedicated men and women who minister to others without hesitation or denominational restraints. In heaven, there will be no denominations—only followers of Christ.

Janice

Once in a lifetime someone comes along who will remain forever in your memory of how that person touched your life and blessed your spirit. Janice, with her bubbly personality and encouraging demeanor, was a person whose smile could light up a room and make everyone want to bask in her presence. For many years she had been a gracious lady in a small town, where she was treated with respect not only by her family but by neighbors and friends. Her affiliation with her church family was very strong, and she was a devoted worker in that congregation. Many times when I came in contact with Janice, I felt that I didn't measure up to her standards; this was my own critical self-assessment because she quickly made me feel at ease in her presence and was always interested in how things were going in my life.

When the hospice referral came for Janice, I felt a piercing of my heart. Her lymphoma had come back with a vengeance and had invaded vital organs. Short of a miracle from God, it would take her life. I knew she had the faith to accept what God had in store for her, and I also knew that if God's plan wasn't completed in her yet, He could heal her until it was done.

As I entered into her bedroom, expecting to bring words of comfort to her, I was surprised when she began to comfort me with the sharing of God's Word. Despite her frail, pale, weakened body and the wig on her head being a little disheveled, her smile radiated that same welcoming spirit that I remembered many times in the past.

The admission paperwork went very quickly with the aid of her devoted family. Both daughters had decided to take family medical leave to care for their mother as she had done so lovingly for them in the past. Her husband could not stay in the same room as we discussed what was happening—they had shared so many good times in their marriage that the thought of life without her was more than he could bear. "It's like cutting my heart out," he said with tears streaming down his face.

"God ease his pain and let him feel Your presence and comfort at this time. Let me be Your vessel to bring peace and comfort through my words and actions," I whispered quietly.

Janice was a matter-of-fact person. "If God doesn't perform a miracle here, then my miracle will be that I get to be in His presence and spend eternity with my son until the rest of my family comes over," she said so beautifully. Her only son had been killed a few years prior in a car accident, and she still felt the loss of his passing. Her family and I prayed for a miracle in her life;

her minister prayed for a miracle in her life; friends prayed for that same miracle, but she continued to decline daily. We were standing on His promise that "by His strips we are healed." I knew in my faith walk that sometimes we are impatient for the healing, but frequently, we just have to stand.

Hospice nurses become part of the family of dying patients when they are blessed to have time to do so, and it was no different in this case. Janice and her family became my extended Christian family. I eagerly looked forward to my time with her because of such an accepting attitude for whatever God had planned for her. It was like she was planning a vacation, only she didn't need to pack any bags or be certain she caught the right flight. I had no doubt that Janice's flight would be right on time, as God planned.

That flight was getting closer to the departure time. I was made aware of this not from my experience of seeing the signs and symptoms of death but from Janice herself informing me in that manner that I had become accustomed to hearing. On Christmas Eve, Janice began to talk with her eyes closed during most of my visit, and occasionally she would say things that I had a hard time comprehending. I listened intently because I knew she was giving me a glimpse into what was waiting for her.

Suddenly, she spoke very clearly. "June, I see my son, Eddie. Am I in this world or the next?" It felt strange for her to ask this question because I was very much alive and ministering care to her, but it wasn't strange to her.

I answered her very matter-of-factly, as she wanted people to do. "No, we both are still here in this world, but if you want, you can let go to be with Eddie."

Her family had told her earlier that she had their permission to go when she wanted. Very calmly, she answered, "No, my grandson is coming home tonight, and I have to wait for him or he will be sad, but I am going to die Christmas morning. Okay?"

Through my experience as an end-of-life care nurse, I've had many encounters with dying persons who would let me know when they were going to cross over. I firmly believed that Janice was going to the Father on Christmas morning. I shared with the family what she had told me and learned that that the grandson was, in fact, on his way home from college to arrive that evening.

The phone rang at a little past eight o'clock on Christmas morning, and I knew who it was before I answered. The family was calling to ask if I would visit and share with the rest of the family for a little time before the funeral home took Janice's earthly body away. She had crossed over at eight o'clock. I was to learn later that the grandson had arrived earlier than expected, and the family opened gifts and shared laughter and joy with Janice before she caught that flight that she knew would be arriving in the morning hour.

This family had looked, listened, and felt what God was showing and revealing to their loved one, and she was able to be blessed as a beautiful, faithful servant, prepared for her heavenly flight.

"But they that wait upon the Lord shall renew their strength; they shall mount up with wings as eagles; they shall run, and not be weary; and they shall walk, and not be faint" (Isaiah 40:31).

Thank you, God, for allowing Janice to touch my life in such a wonderful way.

The belief that God isn't real or that He can't allow glimpses into what the faithful have waiting for them to ease their fear of the unknown causes me to be very sad. I have seen many families argue with loved ones facing death that they aren't seeing what they keep expressing is real. One such case brings me to Harry.

Harry and the Doubting Son

Harry was a very quiet man who worked in his community without others really getting to know him. He and his wife preferred to keep to themselves and rarely invited others to visit. Harry was cordial and gentle in nature but rarely revealed much about his life or his dreams for the future. For some reason, he would visit our family business and do work without hesitation for my husband and my father-in-law. When I would say that he was reclusive, they would say, "You just have to get to know him."

Harry and his wife, Thelma, had one son who rarely visited them; he worked in another state. They rarely spoke about him or what had complicated or hindered this relationship. They would just say, "He is working away." All that was known for certain was that the son was married and was a health care worker in emergency medicine somewhere out west.

Speculation can run wild when one dwells on what might have happened. That speculation soon became a reality to me when, to my surprise, I received a referral for hospice from this very phantom son. He had notified his dad's physician for hospice related to his dad's being diagnosed with metastatic prostate cancer. The son would be present for the admission.

I soon realized that I was going to be second-guessed on most things that I relayed about his dad's disease. It became apparent very quickly into our conversation that he was a professing atheist, and his wife felt the same way. There was to be no conversation about God or attempting to convert anyone. The topic was to be avoided at all costs. What I found interesting was during this intake interview was that Dad rarely said anything. Mom never said anything, allowing the conversation to be centered on what the son and daughter-in-law preferred.

God, how can I reach out to this family? I questioned at each visit. The conversation for the son and daughter-in-law related only to medical questions and how long it would be until death occurred. Most families desire to have everything possible done for their loved one to delay death. This wasn't the case here. I had an uneasy feeling about narcotics in this home environment and became vigilant in counting the amount at each visit. The dad would always say, "My pain is not so bad," but I could see he was walking and moving less and less. When the family was questioned about giving his pain medication on a routine basis, I was informed curtly, "He sleeps too much and has hallucinations too much when he is taking a narcotic. We give them when we think he needs them." This goes against everything a palliative care nurse believes—the patient's self-report of their pain intensity is what controls how much pain medication is to be administered. The son was in the health care system and should have been aware of this.

I learned from dealing with families that occasionally, when there is troubled family dynamics, the caregiver takes control as a way of retaliation against incidents that happened in the past. I did not want this to be the case, but my hands were tied, and it soon became apparent that even the social worker wasn't going to resolve this issue unless the patient himself shared some truthfulness; that didn't happen.

As Harry's disease progressed and he would drift in and out of consciousness, his family would withhold his pain medication, despite education that contraindicated doing so. Harry began to talk frequently during these mind fogs, and often these conversations would be about seeing his brother walking down a path with him into the beautiful woods. Thelma would attempt to listen and encourage him to relay more of what he was seeing because she knew Harry had been extremely close to this deceased brother. A smile would appear on his face, even though his eyes were tightly closed, and a sense of peace would envelope his body. Her attempts to encourage more communication from Harry would soon be squelched by the son or daughter-in-law.

She would attempt to share these visions with me when I visited, but the son, who appeared to be always present, would relay to me that his dad was only hallucinating and was incoherent. I knew differently, as his dad wasn't on mind-altering medication—at their request—and I shared that dying persons often see a loved one in the afterlife who helps make the crossing over so much easier. He was having none of this foolish talk, and my boldness left me.

That boldness returned one day as I was visiting Harry. The son and daughter-in-law had left together to do some business out of town. God always gives an opportunity when it is least expected. I asked Harry if he had a saving grace with Christ and if he was assured of where his soul would go at death. He soon shared that he loved God, but he admitted he hadn't been faithful to Him as he should. When I asked if he wanted his minister to visit so he could be sure of his eternal reward, he quickly agreed.

His minister visited that same day; in fact, he was coming to the home as I left. I knew God had given Harry this time away from his family to assure his salvation. Praise God for answering prayers and giving opportunities.

An injustice was done to Harry, however, because after his death, Thelma wasn't allowed those beautiful memories of what God had revealed to her dying loved one. She looked, listened, and felt, but someone was standing in the way of the blessing that awaited her. It saddened me that his son and daughter-in-law were so closed-minded about what was going on right in front of their eyes; they too could have received a blessing from God. The Evil One used their minds and hearts for his work and was laughing all the time during this illness. Thank God that Harry was given insight into what awaited him, and I pray that our Father allowed his brother to meet him as he crossed over to the other side.

Harry's family missed an opportunity to hear the beauty of what Christ had in store for his faithfulness.

Dana, the Meek-Spirited Beauty

Dana, a meek, soft-spoken young woman, had a smile that could melt any mean-spirited personality with whom she came in contact. Although she never married, she always wanted her makeup and hair fixed just right in case she came upon a "Mr. Right." Her family often teased her about finding someone, but they knew that it would have to be a pretty special man because

Dana had been born with a crippling disability—a disability that made it very difficult to walk without assistance. When she tried, she often fell and injured herself. Most days, she spent time in a chair, reading and watching television, but she was eager and ready to carry on a conversation about current events and the news around town.

Hospice had received a referral on Dana when she was diagnosed with ovarian cancer that had metastasized to the bone and liver—it was too advanced for any definitive treatment. The family was devastated by the news because several cousins were nurses, and they just couldn't understand why nothing more could be done for Dana. The mother was realistic and only wanted Dana to be able to remain at home with her and to be comfortable. I realized that Dana's condition might not be 100 percent pain-free, but I wanted to make it as pain-free as possible.

Over the next two months, Dana's smile never faded when I visited, but she no longer talked about meeting a Mr. Right or that her hair and makeup be perfect. I was grieved to see a bright spot in my life slowing slipping from this world, but I knew that God was waiting in the balance to take her home, where she would be whole and radiant as He had intended her to be.

Unfortunately, one of the major symptoms that she had to contend with in the disease trajectory was projectile vomiting—so violent that it would weaken her until she would collapse in bed for hours. Despite various medications for the nausea and vomiting, it continued daily; not even hospitalization could stop it.

God, I don't understand why she has to suffer this much, I thought. I would pray with her at each visit that the vomiting from the Evil One would be bound in the name of Jesus. Still, it continued. I watched an already thin beautiful body turn into a skeletal shell because she couldn't keep anything of substance down. The family asked about feeding tubes, but the physician advised that this would only cause increased vomiting and risk for aspiration pneumonia. I knew this and had educated them on the benefits and risks of a feeding tube, but they needed to hear it from the physician. This would have only prolonged Dana's disease, and unless God decided to heal her physical body, she was going to die soon.

"And the prayer of faith shall save the sick and the Lord shall raise him up ... and pray one for another that ye may be healed" (James 5:15–16).

Lord, I have prayed this daily for Dana, but she continues to weaken. God must have a reason for not healing her on this side but would heal her at death.

Night after night, she became restless, and the family would call us to ease her distress in whatever way we had been educated to do. One particular night was different; the restlessness was in the form of thrashing about violently in the bed and her sitting up, shouting loudly, "Do you see it?" She kept turning to her mother and saying over and over again, "Do you see it? The light, the light!" After this went on for several minutes, her frail body lay back on the bed, and the restlessness was gone—and the vomiting had disappeared. That radiant smile continued for a few hours, until she slipped into a coma and died peacefully.

She had boldness at the point of death that she hadn't had for her entire life. God allowed that to show through as He was taking her into the light of His eternal rest. Her mother had a glimpse of heaven through Dana's eyes, where ugliness of the disease had been for so many weeks. The family had listened, looked, and felt Dana's passion for thirty years, but they also got to experience a bold passion as she crossed over Jordan to be with her eternal Father. She finally met her "Mr. Right" and was arrayed in beauty that we can only imagine, until we too take that faith journey.

Sally's Near-Death Experience

Many books have been written about documented cases of persons who have had near-death experiences, but I can think of only one experience that I can share for this writing. Many years ago, long before I worked with hospice or specialized working with the dying, I came in contact with a young woman I'll call Sally; she felt led to share her experience. Why she chose me, I am not certain, unless she sensed an openness about my spirit that enabled her to relay an encounter that she had not shared with anyone else, not even her spouse. I had stopped to visit and invite her to a revival at our church, but we began to talk about heaven, with one thing leading to another, until she asked if she could tell me something that had happened to her a few years earlier and why she did not have a fear of dying.

"I don't want you to think I've been hallucinating or was suffering from a nervous breakdown at the time," Sally began, "but it was when I had an operation on my back. I broke my back in a car accident when I was a teenager but delayed having surgery on it because of a congential heart problem that could complicate the operation and recovery. Eventuallly, the pain became so severe that I decided to have the surgery, with the confidence from my physician that things would go well."

With tear-filled eyes, she spoke softly about the incident, stopping frequently to wipe away the tears but then continuing with a driven, determined spirit.

"At some time during the operation, my heart stopped"—she was given full cardiopulmonary resuscitation—"and I found myself above the operating room, looking down, seeing my body being worked on. I was able to see the straight line"—called *asystole*, meaning no heart activity—"on the monitor, as well as hearing everything that was said by the operating room staff. I remember seeing the clock on the wall showing that it was 10:00 a.m."

"Almost instantaneously, I was transported through a long, narrow dark tunnel with a bright light at the end that became brighter as I drew closer to it. The noise was almost deafening as I traveled through this narrow passage. It was noise like multiple voices all speaking at the same time. After reaching the end of the tunnel, I was deposited in a large, beautiful field that had the most vivid flowers I've ever seen, with an aroma that I cannot describe in an earthly language. I saw the image of a being—not sure if was a being but just a glow of a brillant, warm form—that I knew immediately was Jesus. There was a surrounding sound of music that I had never heard before—it enveloped me with love. In the middle of this field was a huge staircase with angels on either side of the stairs."

"While standing at the top of the long, golden stairs, this brillant light form kept motioning for me to climb higher. As I started climbing the stairs, though, I could hear the voices of my husband and daughter, calling for me to climb back down and not to leave them. Halfway up the staircase, I turned and saw my family's faces. I tried to speak to them, but the words would not come—words that would tell them I wanted to stay in this tranquil setting and wanted to continue on toward the light. The light was so loving, and I felt no pain, which I hadn't experienced for many years. I wanted to stay. Once I reached the top of the stairs, the light form spoke—but not in words like we speak here. The lips did not move, but the thought transition was there, clarifying everything that was being said. *'You have to go back—your time is not yet. Your family needs you.'*

"This presence was so awesome and wonderful that I didn't care that anyone else needed me; I needed to be there, but the comforting, loving light form disappeared, and I found myself descending, crawling on my hands and knees back down the stairs. Each stair downward brought excruciating pain that increased with the proximity to the bottom; it was pain on top of the back pain. There was also a spiritual pain that overwhelmed me because I no longer was in the presence of such love and security."

The physical pain that enveloped her was due to the successful code—the medical team had snatched her back from heaven's entrance, which brought with it a slow heartbeat and breath to her body. Transition back to her earthly life brought with it nothing but pain and disappointment. As she related this experience, I never interruped her. She transported me to a glimpse of heaven that was a blessing me and reaffirmed what I knew awaits each believer in Christ.

After many moments of silence, she said, "My life has been forever changed. The thought of dying no longer causes fear, but the thought of getting there without a closer walk with Jesus does increase my anxiety."

I became bold and asked, "Why do you think God let you experience a glimpse into the hereafter? It could only have been the entrance into heaven."

"I have no idea," she answered quietly.

She had mentioned earlier that she hadn't walked close to God for many years, nor had she attended a church with her family. They were such an active and busy family that God and church had taken a backseat. Yes, they believed in God but felt they could make a declaration of faith later in life, when they had more time.

I thought, *Funny how many times I've heard that statement as I stood by a bedside where a loved one was dying and had not committed to the saving Grace of Christ.* Here was one person God had given a rare opportunity to rectify that misbelief.

At the end of my visit, I asked, "Do you want to have a closer walk with the Lord, and could I lead you to that saving grace?"

She declined. This was so difficult for me to understand after such a life-changing supernatural event had happened to her, but before I left, I issued an invitation—we were having a revival at our local church, and I said I hoped to see her there one night.

She didn't say yes nor no. She only smiled and thanked me for listening to an incident that had been on her heart for some time.

As I got in my car, I ushered up a prayer of thanksgiving for that experience that God had opened up to me, and I reminded God that a seed had been planted (as if He didn't already know) but that it was up to Him to unction anything more. I had done all I could do at that point in time.

Immediately, a Scripture came to me from Luke 17:6. "If ye had faith as a grain of mustard seed, ye might say unto this sycamine tree, 'Be thou uprooted and be thou planted in the sea', and it should obey you."

"Well, God, I have planted a mustard seed. Now you remove the barrier and water the seed."

Each night of the revival passed without Sally. Our faith will begin to waver, as it often does, if we reason in the physcial realm, rather than standing firm and letting God work behind the scenes in the supernatural. On the last night, at the last minute before the first song began to play, in walked Sally, and surprisingly, she sat right beside me on the pew.

During the message, which addressed the what-ifs—what if we die without the assurance of salvation, what if we never have time for God, what if we don't know where our eternal home will be—it was almost as if the evangelist had prepared this sermon strictly for Sally, or rather the Holy Spirit had laid it upon his heart to assure a commitment needed to be made by someone who would attend the service.

During the altar call, I knew the Holy Spirit was working in Sally because she was fidgeting like a dying person often fidgets before entering into that restful sleep. But she didn't move forward, and on the final chorus of the final song, I gently touched her hand to let her know I understood. Amazingly, she began to walk forward. The seed was beginning to spring forth a bud.

After that night, I never saw Sally again; she and her family moved to another state, and I later heard that she had died from a heart attack. Sally finally made it all the way into the entrance to her reward. I'm so grateful that her shared near-death experience continues to affirm for me that there is a real place called heaven to which the faithful dying can look forward one day. I had looked, listened, and felt Sally's event and certainly had been blessed by it.

Despite numerous research studies performed by theorists, science has neither disproved nor discredited anything about heaven. I wonder why?

Some theories propose that near-death visions are caused by intense electrical surges or thoughts in our brains when clinical death occurs. These research experiments have been used on clinically dead rats because scientists feel the rat's brain is similar to the human brain. The problem I see with these theories is that the research has not been proven without a shadow of a doubt using a clinically dead human. Most of these research hypotheses determine that this cannot be proven definitely.

Why is it so difficult for the scientific community to realize that even if there are surges of brain activity at clinical death,

God is still in control, and spiritual understanding can't always be proven by scientific facts. There are supernatural facts that can't be explained by research.

First Corinthians 2:9–10 bears repeating: "But as it is written [Isaiah 64:4] eye hath not seen, nor ear heard, neither have entered into the heart of man, the things which God hath prepared for them who love Him. But God hath revealed them unto us by His Spirit for the Spirit searcheth all things, yea the deep things of God."

This Scripture's purpose is to show that we cannot understand the knowledge of God through normal ways of learning, such as research to prove or disprove the workings and thoughts of the dying. At the time of crossing over or almost crossing over, God reveals the rewards that await each dying person. After these near-death experiences, the person always declares that his or her life has been changed drastically. Simply put, the Holy Spirit is the only one qualitifed to reveal what God has in store for the dying person. Why not embrace the beauty of this revelation and use it to prove that there is a higher power, rather than attempting to discredit His exsistence?

The emphasis on advance care planning comes into play more than ever when one has experienced such a life-changing event. Had Sally prepared in advance for her wishes before her surgery, she might have had a different outcome, possibly entering sooner into God's presence for all eternity. But I am grateful that I had the opportunity to hear her story firsthand. Thanks to Sally for the nuggets she planted in my heart.

6

God Does Work Outside the Box

The health care system has been geared for centuries to work with those who are able to speak for themselves. It grieves my spirit to say that one group of people has been ignored, unless those people—the intellectually challenged, those with special needs—have an advocate who is willing to speak for them. In the last thirty years, this population has been brought out of the Dark Ages to where they are no longer placed in an institution because of a physical or mental disability and are no longer treated as non-humans, but society still has a long way to go to embrace them. God has a purpose for all of His creation, and this population has God-given talents that have gone untapped for many years.

Those who are intellectually challenged have mysteries and gifts that demonstrate that God works outside of the box—a box that society has taped shut with insecurities, fears, misconceptions, and biases. My daughter and I have been blessed to have worked with many who have had obstacles to overcome, both physically and mentally, but two of these special people have touched many hearts and lives. Their experiences must be shared so others will see how God uses those whom society has forgotten or cast off as insignificant.

Joshua—"I Already Know"

Joshua was born with a physical and mental disability that required around-the-clock care, for which his dad gladly assumed responsibility after his wife's death. Joshua's two siblings were both professional workers in the health care industry and had very busy lives. When Joshua's dad became too elderly and feeble to care for him at home, it was decided to place Joshua into a group home, where he could receive the attention that he required.

Dad visited daily, and when he was able, he took Joshua out for the day. The brothers would visit occasionally and assumed responsibility as their busy lives would allow. Dad visited less as his health declined, but staff said he would call and speak to Joshua on the phone. Many days, staff would find Joshua in the corner, talking with someone, and when asked who he was talking to, he would answer, "My dad." This seemed to bring him no distress, so staff felt it was one of his voices talking to him. He often heard voices that no one else could hear, and since he had never become violent in any manner, no behavior-altering medications were required.

One day, his brother called and told the staff that their dad had passed away and that they would be in to tell Joshua themselves. Staff became very upset when they learned that the brothers had no intention of taking him to the funeral for that last good-bye to his dad. What an injustice was being done to him. He deserved to be given the option of bidding farewell to the man who had loved him very much and had cared for him for so many years. Were they ashamed of Joshua or unsettled by how he would react in front of their friends and family? Bias and fear were raising their ugly heads again, which only demonstrated that society hasn't come as far as some like to think it has.

Days after the funeral, the brothers came to talk to Joshua and inform him as easily as they could about Dad's crossing over and that he wouldn't be visiting anymore because he had gone to heaven to be with their mom. A clear message from God can come in different forms. As the brothers began to relay the information in the way they had practiced, Joshua immediately told them he already knew that Dad had died. The siblings assumed that the staff hadn't kept the confidence about not sharing this news, but they quickly found out this wasn't the case.

Joshua said, "Dad came to me when he was going away to tell me that he wouldn't be visiting anymore. He had to go to heaven and said he would be seeing me over there soon." In a simple, childlike faith, Joshua was given a glimpse of his dad from God. The family had put God in a box and had tried to protect Joshua from the news (or maybe to protect themselves from embarrassment). He informed them that he was all right and that he could talk to his dad anytime he wanted. God had given him assurance that he was not alone.

What a beautiful gift Joshua had been given from God—a gift that the rest of the family hadn't had the opportunity to experience. Christ loves the infirm, the crippled, and the lame. They are pure, less cynical, and can experience the supernatural that others close out.

I am reminded of Matthew 11:25. "I thank thee, O Father, Lord of heaven and earth, because thou hast hid these things from the wise and prudent, and hast revealed them unto babes."

Supernaturally, God revealed to a babe what would bring him comfort whenever he needed it in the days ahead. We don't understand the mysteries of God, but frequently He lets us have a glimpse of heaven through visions, dreams, and conversations with loved ones who have passed on. I am thankful that we can serve an omnipresent Father who knows just what we need at all times.

Joshua's siblings deprived him of visiting his dad's final earthly viewing, but God showed up and gave Joshua a greater supernatural viewing of his dad. The intellectually disabled don't place God in a box, but they view their Creator as one who can enlighten them when this physical world hinders or forsakes them.

Joe

This incident was similar to Joshua's story, but it adds such credibility to how God uses the less fortunate to bring about supernatural events that it screamed to be shared. Not only does it prove God should never be placed in a box, but it also proves how awesome He is and that unconditional love comes to those when they least expect it.

I am reminded that Christ chose twelve apostles, who were considered poor, lower-class men (fishermen and a tax collector), to be the followers who would change the world. If the common man, rather than a divinely inspired man, had chosen these disciples, the outcome would have been quite different. Status and wealth may have given way to the selection process that could have possibly hindered the entire world's coming to the saving grace of Jesus Christ.

Joe had a severe mental handicap; he often could not carry on meaningful conversations. His care providers knew the meaning of his gestures and body language and could anticipate his needs. They grew to love Joe as if he were family. Those who work with individuals with special needs have been given a special calling from God because the patience and love they demonstrate is easily seen. The same can be said for parents of special-needs children. God knows who has the gifts to love a child who will require more attention than the normal child. Joe was one such child who grew in body but not in mind. As he grew, his parents were no longer able to lift him and do the care that he needed, so they had to place him in a home for disabled adults.

Shortly after Joe's placement into the adult home, his dad passed away suddenly, which made it difficult for his mother to visit, as she required transportation from others. The staff at the adult home became the family for him, celebrating birthdays and holidays, but he continued to have acting-out behavior occasionally and wanted to see his mother. Those visits became less and less frequent until God called her home.

One caregiver, who had a special relationship with Joe and who many times could get him to talk, went in to tell him about his mother's passing. Staff expected that they would have to medicate Joe after the distressing news, but God showed up once again in the most unlikely way—to a man whom society had written off as being unimportant. The windows of heaven opened up for Joe to receive a supernatural blessing.

As the caregiver began explaining that his mother had died, Joe interrupted her, saying as clearly as a man who was a famous orator, "I know. Dad told me." This was surprising to his caregiver, who knew that Joe's dad had died five years earlier. Impossible, he thought, but with God all things are possible. God had allowed Joe's dad to deliver a message so that it would be received from a loved one and allow Joe to know his mother was with him in a place that he would experience one day. Joe then clearly said, "Dad says that he is with Mom and not to worry. Keep looking up, and you'll see us soon."

To this day, Joe continues to talk to his dad, and his acting-out behaviors are less frequent. Through Joe's revealing conversation, which could have come only supernaturally, many of the staff have come to the realization that there is a God and that He cares for every one of us, particularly those who have a pure heart.

It is my earnest prayer that you will come to an awareness that God loves and cares for all His creation, and He will reveal Himself to all who are open to His Holy Spirit. On certain occasions, God opened the windows of heaven to the Old Testament prophets who loved and followed His leading. Why not to the pure in heart?

Second Kings 7:2, Malachi 3:10, and Ezekiel 1:1 demonstrate how God opened up the windows of heaven and poured out his blessing to those who believed. That same promise is for all believers who know and understand the supernatural power of our awesome God.

There is an increase in the number of children being born with the diagnosis of autism spectrum disorder, and when one sees a child with autism, he/she has only seen one with this disability because they are all unique. Just as you cannot put God in a box, children with autism cannot be categorized as all being the same. Often God has allowed these beautiful persons to have the ability to see into the supernatural. I can speak from experience, as I have a grandchild with autism spectrum disorder and have been blessed by his ability to see things in a way that I have never been privy to see. These two persons, Joe and Joshua, were diagnosed with an intellectual handicap, but God used them in a powerful way to impact others. My grandson, Jacob (divinely named), was given to us by God to demonstrate what He wants us to be: humble, accepting, not caring about what others think of us.

Jacob has such an honesty and accepting spirit, a spirit that doesn't have the ability to lie. He has been given the gift to see, without question, that death is only a transition to the other side. His prayers are honest and childlike; if others were able to hear them, they couldn't help but know God hears them and smells them as sweet aroma, just like Jacob of the Bible, when he built an altar and sacrificed to God. Death to a special-needs child is only a passing on to the next life, just as one who gets ready for a trip or vacation. What a wonderful way to look at death—as a transition or crossing over.

Both of my grandchildren were present when their paternal great-grandmother passed on. The elder granddaughter was mature in her thinking, knowing that Great-Grandma was dying. Jacob saw it as Great-Grandmother was going to heaven and found comfort in that realization. After her passing, whenever he had the opportunity to pass her home, he would say, "Great-Grandma died and is in heaven." He said it as a statement of fact. His sadness turned quickly to joy, as God wants us to find in a faithful one's passing. Sadness should turn to joy with a realization that we can be reunited with that loved one who has run the race and kept the faith, as Paul clearly stated in God's Word.

At the time of this writing, Jacob, our grandson, is fourteen years old and can often be heard talking to someone in another room. I have wondered on many occasions if he is talking to Jesus or his special angel who protects him from the ignorance of this world concerning intellectually disabled children or adults. Is God giving him assurance that he is loved and accepted and has a wonderful plan for his life?

Jacob spent several weeks with his paternal grandpa who was terminal from mesothelioma, related to the many years he'd spent in submarines while serving in the navy. At the time of this writing, Don, Jacob's grandpa, has gone on to be with the Lord, but during that transition period, the family got glimpses from him as he shared what was in store for him. Don told his minister that he had seen heaven and knew it was beautiful, and his mom and dad were waiting for him. Many times the caregivers— my daughter, Renee, and her husband, Steve—would hear him talking to someone who was obviously giving him comfort. On one particular occasion, Jacob was sitting quietly by his grandpa and heard him talking to people in the corner of the room. Jacob also looked into the corner, and when questioned what was happening, he calmly said, "I see the two people that Grandpa is talking to. One is Chuck." Chuck had died a couple of years earlier and had a special place of love in the family's heart.

With Jacob's autism, he fears things such as loud noises, spiders, strangers, and many other things, but this incident brought absolutely no fear whatsoever. It was a supernatural event that was normal for him and an event that God allowed him to experience, even as a skeptical scientific population continues to dismiss the supernatural nature of God. When his mother, Renee, shared that she had told Jacob, as his grandpa had requested, that Grandpa would be looking down as one of Jacob's guardian angels from heaven, Jacob simply answered, "Okay." What beautiful childlike faith and understanding God gives to those who are pure in heart.

This childlike faith Joshua, Joe, and Jacob have is a faith that we Christians need to humble ourselves to seek. Thank you, God, for placing those whom others don't understand around me and for letting me see what a blessing they can have on others who open their hearts to them.

"Suffer little children and forbid them not, to come unto Me, for as such is the Kingdom of Heaven" (Matthew 19:14).

When we place God and Christ's Holy Spirit in a confined space, we certainly do not understand the magnitude of God's power. Many religious people use the belief that once someone has left this earth through death, God doesn't use them to bring a peace ever again. I believe that Christ's Spirit brings comfort to us in times of death or bereavement that our human minds cannot understand or comprehend. I certainly believe that we should test the spirits, as God's Word says, but I also believe that God's angels can show up in many forms to relieve that pain that comes from the loss of a loved one. Not only have I experienced it personally (the face of my mother after death, letting me know she was at peace in the bosom of Christ), but others have shared experiences over the years that cannot be explained by the human brain but only through the supernatural power of God.

Angels are all around us, and they often show up during times of extreme stress or fear. One afternoon, my husband was mowing his mother's grass with a lawnmower that caused much anxiety and made his job more time-consuming. His dad, who had died three years prior, had always had the patience of Job when dealing with difficult machinery. My husband has not inherited this patience from his dad. On this particular afternoon, he must have become very impatient or angry at the mower. He looked up and saw a vision of his dad standing against the side of the house, smiling and assuring him that the mower would start if he tried it one more time. He immediately cranked it, and it started. When he looked up again, the image of his dad was gone. Had an angel in the form of his dad—a man who had so many answers for his son and a man that was missed so sorely—shown up? Had God let him see that figure to soothe his stress? I believe He did. God was out of that box that we as Christians often place Him in.

Months before my own dad died, he shared that one of his closest friends had spent the afternoon visiting with him. I knew this man had died years ago, but intrigued, I listened as Dad shared the conversation that he had had with Buckie. Thinking that Dad may have been hallucinating or dreaming, I asked about Buckie's appearance. "Did he have both of his legs?" I knew Buckie was a double amputee and hadn't been able to walk for a long time. Dad wasn't on any mind-altering medications, but I knew in my spirit that this could not have been possible—or could it have been?

Very sharply, Dad answered, "Certainly he had both of his legs, and he walked just fine. He sat in the old rocking chair in the living room that squeaks." Dad began to talk about what a comfort his visit had been and that they had shared the gospel together, as they had in years past.

At this point in Dad's disease, he knew that short of a miracle, he was going to "meet his Maker, as he referred to God. Had God showed up in the form of this man or as an angel in his likeness? I don't know, but I do know that the vision or visit strengthened my dad's faith and allowed his loneliness to dissipate for a short time.

While dealing with a pastor who was a patient of mine many years ago, I had my first encounter with angels surrounding the dying patient's bed. Pastor Floyd had such a peaceful demeanor about him when I ministered to his physical needs. He often would pray for me while I was doing his care—praying that I would have the strength to do my job and have faith that would ease those with spiritual needs. I was blessed to be in his and his faithful spouse's presence.

All dying persons have a life review that can be filled with sadness of loss or feelings of gratitude for what they have accomplished in their lives. Pastor Floyd was no different, but his regret was that he wanted to preach one more service to a group of elderly persons, which he had done for so many years at a local long-term care facility. This would be a major undertaking, and in my opinion, health-wise, it likely would not happen. After the social worker contacted the facility, they were so eager to hear his preaching one last time that they agreed to bring the group to his home.

God is still working and in charge when we don't see how things could possibly work out. One by one, the mostly wheelchair-bound people filed in. It was an image that will always remain with me. This beautiful man, who loved the Lord so much, preached a sermon from his hospital bed, and the tears flowed freely from those who were blessed to be present. I have told so many people in my path that tears are only liquid love. Liquid love surely flowed that day.

I knew Pastor Floyd's goal had been met. A person will usually let go when his or her goals come to fruition. At my last visit with him, he shared that he had angels surrounding his bed, and they were singing the sweetest song to him to make his journey joyous. I would be saddened by his passing for a selfish reason—I wanted to keep his presence with us a little longer, but his work was done, and God was taking him home. I didn't visibly see the angels, but I felt their presence as Pastor Floyd took his final breath. It affirmed that God sends His angels to take His faithful home.

During a bereavement visit with his spouse, she gave me an angel statue as a reminder of what happened that day and that God had blessed us with His angels to assure us that we are never alone. God's angels are always watching and are ready for His call to assist us in whatever capacity we may need. That angel statue has a place of honor in my home, a constant reminder that God uses the dying to bless others if they are open to his leading.

"The people that walked in darkness have seen a great light; they that dwell in the land of the shadow of death, upon them hath a light shined" (Isaiah 9:2).

Through the years, I have been blessed to encounter Christian families who have their act together when it comes to following God's leading and direction of the Holy Spirit in the midst of losing a loved one. It is very difficult when the loved one is a mother who was the center of the family and such a spirit-filled, godly woman that one can't help but question why God didn't heal her physically but chose to heal her as she crossed over. This family has remained close friends and prayer intercessors for my husband and me because of this godly mother who touched my life very briefly.

Blanche was already bed-bound when I received the hospice referral from her physician. This was most unusual because physicians usually delegate this responsibility to a social worker or a staff nurse, but he chose to communicate his wishes for her care. During our conversation, it became very apparent that Blanche was a very special lady to him because he was making home visits to her residence, which is unusual in this day. He wanted her closely assessed for pain and felt that hospice could supply more of her needs than he could, but he still would continue to make home visits.

Upon entering the home of this beautiful lady, I immediately felt the presence of the Holy Spirit. Her supportive family was present and eager to learn what could be done to alleviate her pain and how they could learn to participate in that care. What a joy to know that families still pray and study God's Word, even in the midst of chaos and trials. They knew God was going to help them through this trial and that whatever the outcome, they would be at peace.

Over the months, I became close to Blanche and her daughter, who was the main caregiver. My spirit would leap with joy as I saw the opened Bible on the dining room table each morning. It wasn't placed for my benefit; it was marked and worn from its use as strength and guidance through this storm.

Many prayers went up for healing for Ms. Blanche, but she was content with whatever God had in store for her. Her husband, whom she loved dearly, had gone to be with the Lord many years before, and she continued to grieve his passing and looked forward to the day she would join him. As the months passed, her disease debilitated her more, and she would often see things that most people thought were strange. Those who knew what a faithful woman she was, however, knew God was revealing things to her of what was to come. She had a discerning spirit about who touched her, and on one occasion she asked that a health care aide not return to care for her because she felt the presence of an evil spirit in her. Immediately, another health care aide was assigned, and this presence of discontent left Blanche.

On another occasion, she shared that she saw childlike angels sitting on her dresser, laughing and playing, which brought comfort to her. I believe God was showing her angels' laughter and joy of what she would experience at her passing. She was a woman who had enjoyed joy and laughter with her large family over the years. That laughter would be continued in the eternal home being prepared for her. Although neither her family nor I could visibly see those angels, I know she did. At the time of her death, she passed this life with angels surrounding her bed and family close by, feeling their presence.

I was honored to be allowed to be present at this passing and continue to be honored by the family that she left behind. What a legacy she left to pass on to the next family generation. God had stepped outside of the box that we earthly humans cannot always understand. God's Word says, "With men it is impossible, but not with God for with God all things are possible" (Mark 10:32).

We know from reading God's Word that He used angels to deliver a message or to assist when needed. Why should we expect anything less in times of crossing over? When Christ ascended to His Father, He promised to send a Comforter, the Holy Spirit, with many promises of angelic legions ready to assist the Comforter.

Psalm 34:7 says, "The Angel of the Lord encampeth round about them that fear Him and delivereth them."

There is no greater time for God to send an angel to assist than when He calls a chosen one home. What a glorious thought to know God's angelic host is always waiting in the balance to do His bidding and to help make that transition from this life to the eternal one a comfortable journey.

God's angels can bring messages to those who need a touch from the Master. Weeks prior to my mother-in-law's death in 2005, she shared that on frequent occasions during the night, she felt her husband, Charley's, warm hands massaging her back. Charley died in 1996. This was a practice that he did many nights throughout their marriage when she was extremely tired or anxious. Did God send an angel to prepare her for the journey to join her heavenly Father and her loved one? I believe that He did.

Over the past several years, Larry, my husband, and I have been videoing the services of our church as an outreach to the community. One particular event caused some disagreement as to what needed to be left in or edited out of the taping. This caused us to wonder if God was in this outreach, but we soon got an affirmation that it was something pleasing to Him. One night, a week later, while Larry was the only one up in the balcony where the taping was being done, he felt a comforting hand on his shoulder, reassuring him that truly God was in this outreach. When he turned to see who was touching him, he saw no visible person; he was all alone. Did God send a messenger to alleviate the doubt that we were having concerning this matter? My husband certainly felt that he received an assurance that this was a ministry God was blessing.

Before ascending to be with His Father, Christ gave the Great Commission to his disciples and followers: "Go ye therefore and teach all nations" (Matthew 28:19). We, as followers of Christ, by whatever means possible, must get the gospel of salvation out to those in the community and to the outermost parts of the world. Maybe a DVD bringing the good news is a small step, but we need to be reminded that if Christ used twelve men to change the world, then He certainly can use a DVD to spread His gospel. We can be part of that Great Commission by changing one life at a time.

Although some may be skeptical about angels among us, I believe God's Word is infallible and true. The Word allows us to see many instances where these angelic hosts were utilized for His purpose. I imagine incidents have happened to many people where they entertained angels unaware—where angels aided them in times of danger or encouraged them when they were down or disheartened. How often I have heard an individual say, "I don't know who moved that car out of the way because it was headed right toward me," or "It was only by the grace of God that I didn't wreck."

Many years ago, a close friend and I were traveling home from a day of shopping when a car crossed the center line, and I had time only for the words "Jesus, help us" to escape my lips. With a quick turn of my steering wheel, we came to rest on a wide shoulder of the road. Weeks later, my friend and I, on separate occasions. looked for that wide piece of road but found none to be there. We believe that God sent someone invisible to make that access for us to avoid a fatal accident.

Those who are faithful to reading God's Word will have the affirmation of angels carrying those who are crossing over from this physical life into their eternal life.

The gospel of Luke 16:22 states very clearly, "And it came to pass, that the beggar died and was carried by the angels into Abraham's bosom ..."

This was paradise, where all believers went before the death of Jesus on the cross. Jesus's parable in Luke is telling us that whenever a believer dies, his or her spirit is carried into the presence of God by His angels since Christ's death on the cross. God does work outside the box if we truly will allow Him to do so.

Quite often there are incidents that happen days before dying patients cross over that give insight into how God is going to call them home or a nugget of what they have in store for them immediately after their transition.

Janie and Her Stallion Taking Her to Supper

Janie was 101 years old, but her mind was keen and sharp, and her eyes remained bright, making one wonder if she had a secret that she wasn't sharing. On one particular morning, she very clearly stated that she could see a beautiful snowy-white stallion coming to get her, but it wouldn't come all the way in order for her to climb on. When staff questioned where she was going, she said, with a smile, that the horse was coming to take her to a large dinner. She repeated this story for several days until her family told her that she could get on the stallion and go, if that was what she wanted to do. The next day, she smiled and shouted, "It's coming! It's coming closer, closer!" She took her last breath and crossed over to enjoy the supper that Christ had prepared for this faithful saint.

After her family gave their permission, Janie was able to mount that stallion to go to her heavenly home. What an encouraging moment for those who were left behind. God appears to the faithful aged in very powerful ways. These are vital lessons to be learned by the younger generation. God always saves the best until last, no matter what age they may be when He calls them home. Janie saw a glimpse of what God had prepared for her, and she was carried to it on a white stallion, which she loved in life.

"But as it is written, eye has not seen, nor ear heard, neither have entered into the heart of man, the things which God has prepared for them who love him" (1 Corinthians 2:9).

I believe God has special things in store for us who are faithful in this life—things that brought us godly joy will bring us godly joy in the next life. Many Christians have the misconception that we are going to float around and do nothing all day long in heaven. God created a perfect environment in the garden of Eden that was to be enjoyed by all who kept their faith and obedience in Him, but after sin entered, we had all the fleshy things overcome us—tiredness, illness, sadness, and death.

Janie enjoyed animals, particularly white horses, and I know God wanted to bring joy to her in her last hours of physical life. Who knows? She may be galloping all over heaven, doing spiritual things for her Father. Brings a smile and heartfelt peace, doesn't it?

Ivan—Crossing Jordan

God has allowed me the privilege of taking care of the very young to the very old in times of crossing over, but on one occasion to which I wasn't privy, a nurse shared this story that touched her heart and affirmed her faith of what is out there for the faithful. I had taken care of Ivan weeks before his passing and was impressed by his joy and devotion to his family. He had such humor and often did playful antics that became contagious to all who came into his presence.

Ivan became very restless one night, wanting up and down from his bed, causing his caregiver great distress and tiredness.

His evening nurse had a close attachment to him and was very perceptive to what was going on with the terminal restlessness. Assisting him to stand up, he very boldly began to raise his feet and told her to start stepping into the water. He proudly announced that he was stepping into the Jordan River and needed help getting across. Loudly, he said, "We're almost there." She stepped with him until he became exhausted and lay down in bed to rest. This went on for about a week, until one night, when he finished his walk across the river, he lay down to rest and woke up in eternity.

Ivan's nurse knew this wasn't a foolish request from her patient but one that needed to be completed before he could take his heavenly walk. How wonderful it is when there are nurses or caregivers to assist patients in getting started on that walk. I thank God for this nurse who made our patient more comfortable and eased his discomfort when no other knew what to do. This is what spiritual nursing is all about and is an attribute that many in the health care field need to strive to receive.

Over the years, one of the most important things I have felt confident doing is preparing families for the loss of their loved one, if it becomes apparent that God's desire is to take the loved one home for a spiritual healing. One of the most critical gifts that families or friends can offer for this transition is to make certain the loved one is ready to meet the heavenly Father. Health care workers must learn to be bold in doing this, but first and foremost, they must be faithful followers of Christ and the cross before sharing the good news of eternal life. Those to whom they witness will see fakeness and insincerity in that good news of salvation if the health care workers are not sold on it themselves.

Betty—"Jesus Loves You"

One testimony of sharing the good news is with Betty, the fetal alcohol syndrome patient. Never having the ability to walk or function as a normal child, she was confined to a wheelchair and only able to relate a few words that were understandable to her family and caregivers. Many times, when she became ill, the doctors and nurses felt she wasn't worth receiving care, but I became her advocate. It's amazing what can be accomplished when an advocate is outspoken and bold. Betty brought joy and pleasure to me and her caregivers; God saw her as worthwhile and loved her unconditionally. Through no fault of her own, she was brought into this world with her disabilities. Bad choices made by two alcoholic parents had destined her to the type of life she had to endure.

A devoted aunt cared for her for many years, ever since Betty was three years old, and before long, Betty became the aunt's whole life. But age has a way of slowing the body down, and eventually the aunt no longer was able to care for Betty without outside assistance. God always sends the right people when they are needed to care for the less fortunate, and He didn't do anything less this time. He sent Kristi, a Christian caregiver, to Betty, and Kristi grew to love both Betty and her aunt. How rare that combination is unless God is in the plan. Kristi shared stories with me about how they were doing—by this time, I had changed jobs and no longer had Betty on my caseload. But Betty and her aunt remained precious to me.

Betty's disabilities became life-threatening, and the doctors agreed that aggressive treatment would no longer be beneficial and would cause even more pain for her. Throughout the years that I had been her nurse, I often shared my love of Christ and what He has done for me, but I never knew if the seed had taken root. Church attendance had never been an important part of this family. The aunt wasn't able to drive and never went out of the house unless it was for doctor appointments or hospital visits. But Kristi brought the church to Betty and her aunt. She was able to spend several hours daily with them and often sang and explained frequently how much Jesus loved them.

The gospel of Christ can be brought in different forms—through reading His Word or brought through the lives of others who know of His love. The rubber was meeting the road at this point in Betty's life. The time for crossing over was becoming a reality for her, and despite her having an intellectual disability, God wanted to show her what He had in store for her. In this process, He would show those around her that the windows of heaven would open to a beautiful young creation and that her life was important to Him.

On the day of Betty's passing, her caregiver, Kristi, kept singing and talking about what she had to look forward to seeing. Being in a coma for several days, Betty wasn't able to move or show any signs of understanding what was being said to her. Research has shown, however, that hearing is the last sense to leave the physical body, so Kristi continued to talk to Betty, knowing she could hear what was being said. Kristi told her that when she was ready, it was okay to reach up and take Jesus's hands, adding, "I promise I will continue to look out for your aunt."

Betty, the debilitated, forty-one-year-old, raised her hands toward heaven and crossed over to a glorious party waiting just for her. Kristi knew that God functions outside a box, and she was assured that the moment that Betty grabbed Christ's hand to go from this life to eternal life, she was dancing and talking as she hadn't ever been able to do in this world. Betty will be missed here, but this nurse and many others are looking forward to seeing her whole one day in the future.

Conley—Blind but Still Able to Read the Word

As my car pulled into the driveway of this small rundown home, I felt no fear or anxiety about meeting Conley. I had never been to this part of the county, nor had I any inkling of what awaited me beyond the door. A large, rough-looking, young man opened the door and invited me in. The rooms were dark and very little light was coming through the dirty windows, but what a surprise awaited me in the next room. This brings a cliché to mind: "Don't judge a book by its cover." Upon entering the dreary, drab room, I felt a sense of peace and serenity that can only be explained by the presence of Christ's Spirit in the room. Conley sat in a straight-backed chair that certainly couldn't have been very comfortable for him, but he greeted me with a giant smile and an extended hand. The referral that I had received from his doctor failed to reveal that Conley was totally blind from the disease of glaucoma, which had robbed him of his sight many years ago.

The rough character who answered the door was his only son and caregiver. During the physical assessment, I noticed a Bible on the side table that had its pages taped; they were brown from age. I realized soon that the peace that I felt was probably due to this man being a Christian. As I continued the physical assessment and wound care that the doctor had wanted completed, we began to talk about our faith. Conley quoted Scriptures from the Bible verbatim, as if he were reading them—it was obvious why the Bible was worn and tattered. I asked if I could look at his Bible, and it soon became apparent why he could quote the Scriptures so well. Every page had underlines and markings, so many that the printed words were unclear in many places. He asked me which was my favorite Scripture. I quickly responded that it was Psalm 51:10—"Create a clean heart in me O God and renew a right spirit within me."

Conley reached for the Bible and opened it as though to read it to me. I was astounded that not only did he find a specific chapter and verse, but he also was able to "read" the whole passage that he had chosen without missing a word. I had read in Scripture that God's chosen people were commanded to write His words on their hearts, but this was the first time that I had come in contact with a Christian who had accomplished such a thing.

During my visits with Conley, I soon realized that his time on this physical earth wasn't going to be very long, and I became saddened, knowing that I wouldn't get to enjoy his presence in this life much longer or to have the blessing of his reading to me in his unique way. He became a friend to me and a highlight of my nursing experience due to his blind faith, which made it hard for me to let him cross over to a life waiting for him, where he would visibly see what God had in store for him.

At his passing, I felt a void that was selfish, but I also had such a thankfulness that I was able to be in the presence of such a beautiful man who loved God enough to read His Word to me without seeing. The words were written on and in his heart. Thank you, Conley, for such an awesome lesson.

If I had not had the privilege of working with the dying, I would never have received so many blessings from people who helped form my faith into what it is today. Dying is like taking a one-way vacation, but you don't have to pack a bag to get there. Without that journey by many bedsides, I wouldn't have gotten to know or experience a nugget of what is to come. One such nugget came from a colleague's "Uncle Jimmy."

Jimmy was in the midst of dying but was having difficulty "getting into the boat" to complete the journey. Day after day, Jimmy explained, in his obtunded state, that a boat in a boat kept coming down out of the clouds with two people in the one boat, but the boats never touched the water, which exasperated him and would cause terrible restlessness. His faithful wife of many years would sit daily by his bedside and continue to tell him that he was going to get better, which only appeared to increase the restlessness.

Over the years I have seen a commonality in families, particularly spouses who have been married for many years; they have difficulty telling the dying person that it is all right to go or giving their permission for the dying person to let go. I have witnessed patients who have lain for many days in a persisted vegetative state because loved ones wouldn't verbally release them. I was certain that this was the case with Uncle Jimmy. Families often feel they are giving up if they say "It is all right to go," and it's difficult to allow the words to escape their lips, but it's necessary for the physical well-being of the loved one.

One phrase that brings me consolation and one that I have used with dying patients' loved ones is, "God knows what He is doing when He makes us, and He knows what He is doing when He takes us home." At times, we interfere with His divine will for our lives. Uncle Jimmy's faithful spouse needed to say those words in order for him to be gathered into the boat for his eternal journey across the water. After she released Jimmy with the words, "I love you. You can go," the boat came, and he was assisted into it by one or both of those he had seen for so many days. I am amazed by the means of transportation the dying take to get to their eternal destination. Jimmy was an avid fisherman. Do you suppose that was why a boat came to gather him?

Annie, a retired nurse who looked forward to crossing over to be with her husband, whom she longed for each day, shared a beautiful story of a dying patient to whom she tended many years ago. In the earlier years, the deathbed vigil, whether at home or in the hospital, was isolated to a dark room with closed doors, and when entering the room, the caregivers always spoke in soft whispers, as if to keep secrets from the dying. In one such room, Annie entered to do the physical care and administer the medications needed at the time. All of a sudden, the darkened room became flooded with a bright, blinding light that made it difficult for her to see, but she was able to hear the patient take the last agonal (dying) breath. The bright light immediately left the room when the patient died.

"But the path of the just is as the shining light, that shineth more and more unto the perfect day" (Proverbs 4:18).

These words take on an even greater meaning when one experiences the supernatural with those that are dying. There is a clearer understanding of Christ being our light in the midst of the darkness.

7

Affirmation—Where Do I Go from Here?

Nurses have golden opportunities to become blessed by working with the dying. It's a calling that many in the health care system shun because they do not truly understand the process or don't fully realize that at some point in time, all persons will die. There is no part of health care that doesn't have to deal with the care of a dying patient, from obstetrics to palliative care. The continuum is vast, with so many missed chances to comfort those going through this process or to support the families that experience this journey with their loved ones. Who better to look to for guidance and comfort than a compassionate, faith-believing nurse?

So many experiences have been gratifying to me in my nursing career. I've shared a few examples to affirm that eternal homes await us, whether it is a home of unrest or a home of peace and serenity.

I am so grateful that dying is no longer seen as a failure to many in the health care field but rather a challenge to ease the discomfort of that process, whether spiritually or physically. It is easier to work aggressively on the physical discomfort of the dying, because with the specific medications and use of adjunct alternatives, that discomfort can be eased with the right knowledge and appropriate regime. The spiritual pain is altogether different and proves many times to be the most difficult to recognize and to alleviate. This requires a health care worker—whether physician, nurse, or others who work in this particular field—to be very perceptive and intuitive to what is happening to the patient, as well as to the family of the dying loved one.

I often compare the journey of labor and delivery with the journey of death and dying. Births and deaths are occasions that prompt different emotions for different people. Most births cause emotional joy, whereas death evokes the sense of loss and sadness. Why is this? Both should initiate a sense of accomplishment and a sense of celebration if the event is expected and there is an assurance of where the loved one will reside. Many might assume such a statement was made by someone who has not experienced either significant event or someone who was cynical and pessimistic, but this certainly is not the case.

In my lifetime, I have had the blessings to share both of these experiences and look at them as one and the same. Why is it that everyone jumps for joy and has such a feeling of warmth and fulfillment at the birth of a child who is coming into an unknown world, where many events may have a positive or negative impact on this small one's life?

Many children are brought into this world without a thought of the what-ifs or to the preparations for being a dad or mother to this precious one that God gave them the responsibility to raise. If the earthly dad had the same attributes as our heavenly

Father, then the destination would be a blessed occasion and a journey of promise.

Preparation for the delivery of a baby comes in many forms—parents/grandparents, classes, books, articles, or simply with the "luck of the draw" of nature The destination is already decided for the child, and he or she has no say as to where that is going to be. It might be to a loving family (biological or adopted) or to an abusive family, where the pregnancy may have been conceived out of lust or rape. There is no user manual appropriate for all, only a manual written by someone who has experienced this process in the past and has taken the time to write it down.

During labor and delivery, a coach is usually present—the dad, parent, sibling, or a significant person of choice—to guide the expectant mother through the process of birth. A physician and/or nurse will be present to assist with a successful outcome and to explain what is happening at various points in the delivery. These points can be difficult, traumatic, painful, or easy and peaceful, depending on how much preparation and information the expectant parents have been given.

At death, we are faced with many of the same challenges as the birthing process—where the destination will be (heaven or hell) and whether the voyage getting there is going to be a positive or a negative trip. A major problem is that the dying are often assisted by well-intended but ill-prepared coaches to guide them through their death and dying journey. Well-intentioned coaches may demonstrate a lack of understanding of what is happening or may only know one avenue to tap into, which can cause chaos and stress, not only to the patient but to the family as well. This is where the knowledge, power, and beauty of a palliative care or hospice nurse intensifies when that nurse is also a faith-filled Christian. The patient and family have the best of both worlds—a physical and a spiritual preparatory coach for the event. A faith-believing palliative care nurse has the best coaching manual, one that has stood the test of time and never goes out of date: God's Word. Along with this manual and the knowledge of death and dying, she or he assists the patient and family throughout a difficult process, answering questions and informing them every step of the way to reach the ultimate destination.

Faith-filled families rejoice for their loved one at the end of this physical journey, with the assured hope of a supernatural home, where this saint is gathered in and never has to experience the sting of death ever again.

"Death is swallowed up in victory. O death, where is thy sting? O grave, where is thy victory?" (1 Corinthians 15:54–55). Those faithful to the end will not experience a spiritual death, only the crossing over from life to life.

I would be remiss if I didn't share my firsthand knowledge of how some of these well-intended friends cause undue stress at a time when a patient (coherent or not) or families (Christian or not) need guidance that will ultimately change the course of a dying journey. I want to reiterate a few of the experiences mentioned previously that have caused me to look at the "religious"(all-knowing about God and His ways) in a new light. I call it a "Pharisee faith."

I have heard statements such as "You must have not asked for forgiveness and have a sin in your life, which is why you are sick and dying. You don't have enough faith or you would be healed." Remember Job in the Bible and his well-intentioned friends? Job knew he was right with God. I believe these "friends" were allowed in God's Word, though they were wrong, to show us that circumstances often do not present the true picture. Understanding this, we should withhold judgmental statements. God's Word stated that Job was a perfect man, and God was pleased with his faith. But we also find in the Scriptures that Job did not have one person to stand up for him except God. This is a powerful lesson for those who make comments that judge others at a crucial time in their lives, especially things about which they know little or nothing.

Other piercing statements are "You must be paying for the sins of your family," or "You just don't have enough faith, or you would be whole and healthy." They quote the Scripture that says, "I would that you would be in good health and prosper," which is what God's Word says. "God's Word says you are supposed to live three score and ten," they say, which also is true, but there is that lack of understanding again.

It is difficult to comprehend why a beautiful, innocent, and pure five-year-old child like Olivia had to die prematurely. Simply put, it is a lack of understanding of God and His ways. Our understanding may not always be God's purpose. Well-intentioned friends can damage many faithful dying persons and families with hurtful remarks, causing them to question why this is happening to them. Sometimes we cannot explain these events, but we can only stand firm in the time of trials and testing.

"Therefore, my brethren dearly beloved and longed for my joy and crown, so stand fast in the Lord ..." (Philippians 4:1). Our understanding will come by and by and in God's time. Until that time, we just stand.

For many years, there have been two areas of health care that have not been very appealing to the health care worker—working with the mentally ill and caring for the dying. Just like those with mental disabilities, the dying were many times placed in darkened rooms with very little or no interaction from the outside world. Despite the strides we have made in these two areas of health care over the past twenty years, there are still many physicians and nurses who feel the dying patient is a sign that they have failed or that there is no longer hope for those who are at the end of life. I am certainly reminded that there is always hope until the last breath is taken, and even then, there is still a greater hope—the hope of eternal life.

As I reflected over the stories I've shared in this writing, I was reminded of how my own walk of faith has been affirmed with a newness and an anticipation of looking ahead to what will be in store at my own crossing over. I'm not in a rush to experience this process, but as I become older (and, I hope, wiser), my thoughts turn more to that journey. After standing by so many bedsides and getting just enough insight into the unknown to pique my curiosity of what is waiting in the balance, a warm feeling burns inside of me to know more.

Many have asked what I have learned through these experiences of caring for the dying. The answer comes very easily—there is an affirmation of faith and a confirmation of something greater to be experienced after this physical passing. So many patients have shared those supernatural moments with me and blessed me in a way that words cannot describe.

Writing about these experiences has been cathartic and embraces the celebration of lives who gave meaning to my work and to my faith. I contemplate what means of transport I will be shown when the time arrives for me to cross over. Will it be a boat, as Conley saw coming for him, or will it be Janie's beautiful white stallion, or my own personal angel to carry me? By whatever means, a glorious reunion will take place with loved ones who have gone before me.

The most important lesson I have learned is that there is no need to be afraid if we are going through that process as a faithful servant to the Lord. Our faith in this life is what assists us in that passage to our eternal home. I am reminded of the beautiful words: "Knowing that he which raised up the Lord Jesus shall raise up us also by Jesus and present us with you ... For which cause we faint not; but though our outward man perish, yet the inward man is renewed day by day ... While we look not at the things which are seen, but at the things which are not seen: for the things which are seen are temporal; but the things which are not seen are eternal" (2 Corinthians 4:14, 16–18 NIV).

It is my hope that if you have been skeptical about the windows of heaven opening up and giving supernatural glimpses into what is waiting for God's saints that you will step back and be open to hearing great life-changing accounts from dying patients or dying loved ones. Rather than being depressed while working with the dying, be challenged that you are about to be blessed. Real opportunities are available to nurses and caregivers who are unsure whether there are real places called heaven and hell— opportunities to get a glimpse into those worlds.

Adrenaline flows when an ambulance siren blows and the responders are uncertain of the challenges that call may bring. The same is true for emergency situations where nurses and other health care workers are extremely vital to saving the traumatized or critically ill. The terminally ill patient who takes that last physical breath is just as vital and as challenging. After that last breath, eternity begins. That travel to eternity is one that every person must journey, unless Christ returns for His faithful first; this eternity will bring about changes for all humankind.

I am in a place of contentment and peace but realize that nursing doesn't end with retirement; it only opens up new doors to spread my experience to others, whether through educational classes or by assisting caregivers in the transitional stages of the end of life for a loved one. Many times, just having someone to understand and educate the caregiver on what is happening and what to expect is the greatest gift to give to another.

While working with the terminally ill, I have come to value and appreciate caregivers who support those individuals who will be crossing over soon. This is a challenging and tiring job, particularly when there is only one caregiver to supply the needs to keep a loved one comfortable, both spiritually and physically. Some families that already are dysfunctional become even more dysfunctional at these critical times, when decisions have to be made. When quarrels and bitterness become a normal way of caring for the dying person, the loved one may feel like a burden; the appetite diminishes and the terminally ill individual becomes withdrawn.

One very important step to help alleviate these nightmares and decisions in dealing with the affairs of an individual at the end of life is advance care planning. Some people, particularly Christians, do not want to discuss decisions concerning their deaths, as this is perceived as giving up hope of a cure for the disease or a lack of faith that God can heal them. Family members may have those same concerns and will not discuss them until it becomes necessary, as they are afraid that their motives may be misconstrued. Conversations about these decisions are so much better discussed earlier rather than later. God is always a healer, but there are times when pain overwhelms the body so much that there is a welcome release at death and a yearning for the spiritual healing. The crossing over from death to life—or as I like to express it, from life to life—is a friend if we know Jesus Christ. Heaven is our intended true home; this earthly one is only temporary.

"But now they desire a better country, that is, an heavenly, wherefore God is not ashamed to be called their God for He hath prepared for them a city" (Hebrews 11:16).

Advance care planning is a way of assuring that one's wishes and choices at the end of life are carried out; it spares prolonged periods of suffering and eases family members' burden of having to make difficult choices—decisions that they may not all agree upon. So often, expenses and the emotions involved in these hasty decisions can be astronomical and may cause rifts in families that never will be bridged. Most important, the true choices of the loved one may be ignored because they were not put in writing.

When advance care planning is completed early in life, whether through a living will, a medical power of attorney, or a Physician Orders for Scope of Treatment form (POST/POLST), a physician-signed order form that communicates and puts into action treatment preferences for patients who are nearing the end of life), the burdens are taken off of loved ones, and it becomes a final gift that the family can give, knowing that those wishes will be respected.

The individuals discussed in this book were fortunate to have had advance care planning through their own initiatives or through the efforts of a hospice program. At times, getting all family members on board with advance wishes wasn't always easy, particularly if the loved one was actively dying upon admission and health care facilities had failed (or attempted but failed) to get these documents completed before discharge. Not only did families have to come to terms with the approaching loss, but the added burden of what their family member may or may not have desired was an added complexity.

The day will come when everyone faces old age, if the Lord tarries His return. Many younger adults state they are too young to worry about such things and they will get around to it later. If this is the case, I encourage that these documents be completed for them and for their aging parents so that there will be less of turmoil when decisions are needed. As you've read in this book, many were young when God called them home.

Be bold and ask God for wisdom to have the right time and a right place for such discussions. God honors those who do everything in His name with respect and love.

"But the wisdom that is from above is first pure, then peaceable, gentle and easy to be intreated, full of mercy and good fruits, without partiality, and without hypocrisy" (James 3:17).

A word of caution: making end-of-life choices for yourself is not easy, but leaving them for someone else is risky and burdensome. Whenever these decisions are made, with a firm faith in Jesus Christ there will be a peace that your house is in order to allow for the heavenly ride.

"And the prophet Isaiah, the son of Amoz came to him and said unto him, Thus saith the Lord, Set thine house in order; for thou shall die and not live" (2 Kings 20:1).

Hezekiah had a different outcome after prayer and did not die at this time, but I believe God's Word tells us that we need to have our houses in order when preparing to die.

A last will and testament is usually completed because we want to be assured that our families will inherit what is rightfully theirs or for financial gain and everything is in order, but the living will or medical directive is often overlooked as insignificant. If these two documents are not completed, many times the financial gain that the last will and testament brings at the passing may be depleted by choices the patient may not have wanted or would not have chosen, had the patient been coherent or put choices in writing.

If you have not considered advance care planning for yourself or a loved one, I encourage you to do so to assure those wishes are made known. Everything is better when written down, which alleviates conflict over what the family members heard their loved one say he or she did or did not want. Confusion only arises when those wishes are interpreted by various family members without a written medical power of attorney document.

The most stressful situations that hospice and palliative care teams face are when the child from out of state, who has not been involved in Mom's or Dad's care, rides in on his or her white horse to save the day—or rather to "save" Mom or Dad from the process of dying. Accusatory statements often are made to the health care workers or to the other family member caregivers about their letting the parent die without trying everything possible and without having a sound knowledge of what has been attempted or what has become futile for the dying loved one. This is when advance care planning becomes imperative and a course of care can be charted for the newly involved family member. Demands from the formerly absent family member often result from guilt for not having been involved sooner or an attempt to make up for dynamics of the past.

Hospice and palliative care nurses have to wear many hats when dealing with the dying patient and with the family who is dysfunctional in this journey. Firmness and boldness are two important characteristics needed for a successful transition. Many times this boldness and firmness is met with opposition and anger, but a well-experienced nurse, social worker, or clergy in the field of death and dying will recognize what needs to be addressed to make this crossing over a positive one. Every aspect of the physical, psychosocial, and spiritual component must be looked at and discussed as a team before the issues can be resolved. The family and patient (if able) must be part of that team; otherwise, dynamics can and will get out of control. An added asset is when those on the team have a faith based in Christ. The resolutions come quickly when faith takes priority in the journey.

So, where do I go from here? I continue to have vigor and have set goals and challenges to help others in need by educating families about the dying process and assisting inexperienced nurses about this area of nursing that is so often overlooked in health care. God has blessed me with many years of experience, and the knowledge cannot lay dorment in my heart. I must impart it to others who are experiencing difficult times with a dying loved one's crossing over.

The writing of this book has been a primary source of sharing how important it is for health care workers to give appropriate attention to the dying person's care and to pay particularly close attention to what the dying person shares as he or she transitions to the other side. My life will never be the same, and I can answer quickly when asked how I can work with the dying for so many years.

It is my hope that you will draw strength from this book and realize that crossing over is a part of life that we all must face sooner or later, unless Christ returns before that crossing. The Scripture says it so well:

> There is a time for everything, and a season for every activity under heaven. A time to be born and *a time to die* a time to plant and a time to uproot, a time to kill and a time to heal, a time to tear down and a time to build, *a time to weep_*and a time to laugh, *a time to mourn* and a time to dance, a time to scatter stones and a time to gather them, a time to embrace and a time to refrain, a time to search and a time to give up, a time to keep and a time to throw away, a time to tear and a time to mend, a time to be silent and a time to speak, a time to love and a time to hate, a time for war, and a time for peace." (Ecclesiastes 3:1–8, emphasis mine)

This beautiful piece of Scripture covers the entire circle of life and emphatically states that there is a time and season for each of us to go through. Notice the parts that I emphasized—a time to die and a time to mourn. These are the areas in this physical world that we experience until we depart this life to what God has in store for us to receive as rewards. Then peace, joy, and understanding will become obvious at this passing.

One of the most profound quotes that I have ever read comes from Rabindranath Tagore, a Bengali poet and philospher: "Death is simply putting out a candle because morning has come." All who cross over in faith no longer need the candle because morning has come; Christ will be the light. That is why I feel certain that the dying loved one who has a strong faith always sees a bright light to guide the way home.

There will always be skeptics and a scientific community that try to disprove this theory of life after death, but those of us who have spent years of working with the dying will emphatically say they are so wrong. One day, they too will experience death, and their closed minds will be opened by what is waiting for them at that final breath. I have had many say that they don't believe there is anything after death, and I always answer, "But what if there is? Then it will be too late after you have taken that last breath and entered eternity."

After reading these simple stories, I hope you anticipate death as a journey to the unknown with a promise of joy and peace with no pain or sorrow. That death will not produce fear as you (or a loved one) travel this path; it will be a journey with boldness and determination that you know the best is yet to be. The personal insights that I have shared in this book are only a few that were worthy to relate. Other deaths were sometimes unexpected and there was not enough time to get to know the patient or families. Frequently, this was due to physicians not wanting to give up on doing aggressive treatments or because of demands from families to keep trying procedures that were futile. Ultimately, the outcome was the same: death. This is very frustrating for a palliative care team because they are denied the privilege of bonding and being enlightened by the loved one's journey.

Often, the journey of crossing over is already happening when the loved one is discharged from the hospital. Admission paperwork and treatments become paramount for the physical pain, rather than for the spiritual outcomes—there just isn't time. This brings sadness to my heart because I realize that those glimpses into the afterlife were missed in the busyness of the hospital setting. This is no reflection on the hospital staff; there simply was not time or knowledge for staff to secure what needed to be completed for this transition to the other side.

Many transitional journeys happen with the person or persons the dying loved ones want to be present—those they know, who will understand and be strong for the rest of the family. Others cross over when no one is present because of dignity issues, and they want to spare those closest to them from seeing that last breath. I have seen examples of both and have seen the guilt and experienced the anger of those who wanted to be present but were not. There is one last incident that I feel is important to share. ...

Buddy and His Girls

Buddy comes to mind as one person who chose when to let go and chose whom he wanted present at that passing. He had been blessed with a beautiful wife and twin daughters. One daughter was strong and able to share in the care of her dad, while the other was nervous and anxious most of the time in his presence. Both loved their dad in special ways but somehow a little different. Buddy had been a vibrant man in his late forties when he contracted ocular melanoma (cancer of the eye) that had metastasized rapidly. He was a blonde haired, blue eyed man with very fair skin.who had served in the Navy. He had spent many months on a ship that had intensified his already at-risk skin. I soon learned that Buddy liked to spare his family this dying process as much as possible, but the older twin (by two minutes) was adamant that she would be sharing the time with her dad and be present when he died. The younger twin expressed the same desire.

Even in the dying process, a parent tries to shelter a child he or she feels cannot handle the moment of letting go. Buddy was that type of parent because he often shared with me that he did not want the younger twin present at his death because of her fragile state. The day of Buddy's crossing over, I had the privilege of being present and recognized the symptoms. I knew it wasn't going to be long before his Creator would bring him home. He looked up at the younger twin and asked her to go to the store and get him a special drink that he was craving, despite his inability to swallow for the past several hours. His voice was only a whisper, but Tracy understood it and was glad that she could still do something positive for her dad. She had barely left the driveway when Buddy looked up, smiled, and went home. He was still doing his last protective task with a daughter he knew would not be able to accept his passing.

Tracy displayed guilt and anger when she was called back before she had even made it to the store. This was not a task that I relished doing, but she had to know that those who pass often choose the time of letting go, as well as who they want present at that time. I hoped this explanation eventually eased Tracy's pain and separation.

The same is true of individuals' grief and how long they grieve. Although the task is often left to a bereavement coordinator or the clergy, a pallative care nurse who has had a strong bond with the family may be called upon to follow up. I realized a long time ago that individuals handle dying differently, and just as one cannot put God in a box, the bereaved cannot be placed in a "one size fits all" category. The most important attribute for breavement is the power of presence; just being there to listen. As I have shared many times, I feel that tears are only liquid love. The faithful know God's Word says, "Put thou my tears into thy bottle" (Psalm 56:8). What a comfort this piece of Scripture brings to the faithful's mourning.

The best advice this palliative care nurse can give to those working with the bereaved is this: don't expect certain behaviors that you might have learned from a book, and don't be quick to relay how you responded to a similar loss. Each loss is different. This has been a learning concept for me—it took many years to realize that there isn't a set way to grieve. Just be present and listen.

The past twenty-five years of working with the dying not only has affirmed my present faith, but it also has strengthened that faith by the glimpses into the destination that I will be taking one day. When I transistion from here, I probably will have two of the same concerns that the dying so often share with me: fear of dying in pain and concern for the journey of getting there. Many also have a fear of dying alone, despite a few patients saying that is their desire. I encourage other health care workers to see that the dying loved one isn't alone. Over the years, I have spent many hours by the bedsides of dying patients when a loved one could not be present.

I know where I will go from here, so when my time for crossing over comes, my one final desire is that I will be blessed to have a faith-filled nurse who will alleviate these concerns by the choices that she or he makes in my care, as well as assuring that my spiritual needs will be assessed and honored. This is what every dying person deserves but so often doesn't have the opportunity to experience.

A few of the incidents in this book have changed my outlook on life. I wanted to end with a poem I wrote that expresses my gratitude for standing by those dying patients' bedsides and what that has meant to me through the years. I pray that you will be encouraged and strengthened by my experiences, and when your crossing-over time comes, I pray that you too may have an impact on those left behind.

Crossing-Over Blessings

When my earthly work is done
And my race down here is won
I'll have a life review
Of those who blessed my life
Of patients crossing over
And families without strife.

I'll smell the sweet perfume
Of heaven's purest air
Because you shared it years ago
As you were crossing there.

Crossing over—it's never done alone
Guardian angels will descend
Snatching the faithful upward
Forever to their home.

The music will be so grand
You shared this too
There will be angelic hosts
Appointed to sing me through.

The light of love from others
Will soon be left behind
But I'll connect with Jesus
Who loved me all the time.

Loved ones will greet me there
Because you told me so
With smiles from Mom and Dad, our baby
Who didn't get to grow.

Father, how can I repay you
For sharing oh so much
To this unworthy servant
Who felt the Master's touch?

You allowed me to be present
For times of need and stress
To ease the journey homeward
For their joy, peace, and rest.

Thanks God for the openings
To let Your glory through
To the many faithful patients
Who glorified me too

My nursing was a blessing
Because of faith in thee
I know I have Your promise
The best is yet to be!

CPSIA information can be obtained
at www.ICGtesting.com
Printed in the USA
BVOW07*2304300416

446012BV00001B/1/P